THE HISTORY

OF

FOURTH ARMOURED BRIGADE

The Naval & Military Press Ltd

Published by

The Naval & Military Press Ltd
Unit 5 Riverside, Brambleside
Bellbrook Industrial Estate
Uckfield, East Sussex
TN22 1QQ England

Tel: +44 (0)1825 749494

www.naval-military-press.com
www.nmarchive.com

In reprinting in facsimile from the original, any imperfections are inevitably reproduced and the quality may fall short of modern type and cartographic standards.

FOREWORD

I have written this history in order that past and present members of 4th Armoured Brigade may have a record to remind them of the five years of fighting the brigade has seen. I cannot in this short account attempt to give a true picture of that time. That I hope will be provided by the memories which this record may recall. Much of it is taken from the personal memories of myself and others who took part in the campaigns or from the War Diary. I am indebted to Capt. A. MacLennan, RA, GSO 3 of the Brigade since January 1943, for the material for Chapter IV, Sicily and Italy. It is as accurate an account as I can write without becoming involved in a great deal of research. If inaccuracies are found, I hope they will be forgiven. I have not included any maps, as so many would be needed.

HQ
4th Armoured Brigade
Germany
July, 1945

R. M. P. Carver,
               Brigadier.

THE HISTORY OF FOURTH ARMOURED BRIGADE

CONTENTS

Chapter I. The first year. Defeat of the Italians 5
January 1940 to February 1941

Chapter II. Tobruk. Relief and Loss 9
May 1941 to July 1942

Chapter III. Fourth Light. Alamein to Tunis 14
July 1942 to May 1943

Chapter IV. Sicily, Italy and Home 19
June 1943 to June 1944

Chapter V. Liberation. France, Belgium and Holland 27
June 1944 to February 1945

Chapter VI. Into Germany to Victory 36
February to May 1945

Appendices

    A. Brigade Commanders 44

    B. Units of the Brigade 45

CHAPTER I

The First Year — Defeat of the Italians — January 1940 to February 1941

When the "Mobile Division (Egypt)" was formed after the Munich crisis in the autumn of 1938, it consisted of a Light Armoured Brigade, the old Cairo Cavalry Brigade, a Heavy Armoured Group and a Pivot Group. The heavy Armoured Group consisted of the 1st and 6th Royal Tank Regiments. In January 1940 Mobile Division (Egypt) was renamed 7th Armoured Division, the Light Armoured Brigade became 7th Armoured Brigade and the Heavy Armoured Group became 4th Armoured Brigade. Lt-Col. H. R. B. Watkins, who had been commanding the Heavy Armoured Group, was succeeded in command of 4th Armoured Brigade by Brigadier J. A. L. (Blood) Caunter, DSO, MC, who had commanded 1st Royal Tank Regiment from 1934 to 1939. The brigade was at the time in Main Barracks at Abbassia, having returned from the desert near Mersa Matruh at the end of November 1939, when it was clear that Italy was not at that time going to declare war against us.

Soon after its birth the organization of the brigade changed: 1st Royal Tank Regiment went to 7th Armoured Brigade, 7th Hussars from 7th Armoured Brigade taking their place. At that time 6th Royal Tanks had about a dozen A 9 medium tanks, the forerunner of the Valentine: all the rest of the tanks of the brigade were light tanks, mostly Mark VI and Mark VI B. There were not enough two-pounder guns for all the A 9s nor enough machine guns, though most of the tanks managed to be equipped with at least two out of their full complement of three.

In February General Wilson held two large scale exercises, in the first of which the brigade took part. The A 9s were brand new and had not been run in: there were no spares in the country. However HQ British Troops in Egypt insisted that they should take part in the exercise, with the result that almost every one siezed up.

In April it became clear that the Italians were viewing warfare with a more favourable eye. 11th Hussars and the Support Group moved up to the area of Sidi Barrani and Mersa Matruh, followed in the second week of May by 4th Armoured Brigade, which concentrated just south of Gerawla. On the night of 10/11th June, when war against Italy was declared, 11th Hussars and the Support Group moved up to the frontier, 4th Armoured Brigade moved at first light on June 11th by the desert track known as the "Road to Rome" to the area later known as "Conference Cairn", on the top of the escarpment southeast of Halfaya. 11th Hussars, supported by 4 RHA, had already captured Sidi Omar. The brigade's first action was the attack on Fort Capuzzo. The attack was preceded by naval and air bombardment and was a complete success: those tanks, which were lucky enough to have guns, bombarded the walls of the fort. By modern standards it was a primitive, almost mediaeval scene. It served one great purpose in that it gave every man in the brigade a hearty contempt for the enemy, and instilled a fear of our armoured forces into the Italian Army, from which they never recovered. The capture of Capuzzo was followed by a period of aggressive patrolling, of which the main burden was borne by 11th Hussars. At the end of June 7th Armoured Brigade relieved 4th Armoured Brigade, which then concentrated near Mersa Matruh. In the late summer it was joined there by the rest of the division, less the Support Group. It had become clear that the Italians, who had re-taken Capuzzo in July, were planning a further advance, and it had become essential to restrict the mileage of our antiquated tanks which were fast wearing out. In the middle of September the Italians advanced with great pomp and ceremony as far as Sidi Barrani, harried by the Support Group, 4 RHA in particular causing them great annoyance. Having reached Sidi Barrani the Italians began to build perimeter camps in a ring from east of Sidi Barrani at Meiktila, through the Tummars and Nibeiwa to Alam Rabia, the Sofafis and Halfway House to Halfaya itself.

While Jock columns of the Support Group harried these camps and prevented the Italians from closing the gap near Bir Enba between the camps at Nibeiwa and Alam Rabia, the brigade was getting stronger every day. More A 9 and A 10 cruisers were becoming available. 6th Royal Tanks now had two squadrons of cruisers and one of lights, and 7th Hussars had one cruiser and two light squadrons. In November 2nd Royal Tanks complete with A 13 cruisers, the forerunner of the Crusader, and 3rd Hussars complete with lights joined 7th Armoured Division, having been sent out in advance of the rest of 2nd Armoured Division. 2nd Royal Tanks less one squadron with one squadron of 3rd Hussars under their command joined the brigade, a welcome addition. One battery of 1 RHA also came under command, the first gunners to become a permanent part of the brigade.

On December 8th the brigade moved forward from the Matruh — Siwa Road to the area of Piccadilly. Early on the following morning, while 4th Indian Division supported by 7th Royal Tanks with their Matildas attacked Nibeiwa camp, the brigade slipped through the gap on their left, which Support Group with 4 RHA had done so much to keep open. With hardly a pause the brigade went straight through behind all the camps to cut the coast road west of Sidi Barrani, where it was firmly established by last light. By this bold move the large enemy forces in Nibeiwa, the Tummars, Meiktila and Sidi Barrani were completely cut off. The brigade stayed in that position roping in crowds of prisoners, while 4th Indian Division attacked and cleared in turn the camps to the east and 7th Armoured Brigade struck through to the west to Buq Buq, where it was almost engulfed in the crowds of prisoners. Leaving 6th Royal Tanks to help 4th Indian Division capture Sidi Barrani itself, the brigade then turned south again to Bir Enba and swept through the desert, chasing the Italians fleeing from Rabia, the Sofafis and Halfway House into Bardia itself. By-passing Sidi Omar and Sollum, the brigade went straight to cut the main road from Bardia to Tobruk a few miles west of the perimeter of Bardia defences. This swift, bold stroke produced strong reaction from the Regia Aeronautica, which made life very unpleasant, and also strained the Q resources almost to breaking point. 5 Coy RASC drove day and night without stopping, collecting captured petrol from Sidi Barrani and delivering it to the much-bombed brigade B echelon, who were kept going by the tireless energy of the late Brigadier (then Major) George Webb.

Support Group, having captured Sollum, relieved the brigade west of Bardia. After coming back to the frontier to reduce the garrison of Sidi Omar, the brigade concentrated just west of Capuzzo, while 6th Australian Division came up to take Bardia. Christmas was celebrated here on half a pint of salty water a day and bully and biscuits.

The attack on Bardia began on December 27th: as soon as its success was sure, the brigade moved west along the Trigh Capuzzo to El Adem, where the pile of ruined aircraft bore witness to the effective work of Air Commodore Collishaw's gallant little Desert Air Force, and drove the enemy inside the perimeter defences of Tobruk, while 7th Armoured Brigade and Support Group completed its encirclement to the west.

As a result mainly of mechanical troubles and the complete lack of spares, it now became necessary to re-organize the brigade. 6th Royal Tanks were therefore dismounted, and, much to their chagrin, had to return to Alexandria, their tanks being handed over to the other two regiments. On January 22nd 6th Australian Division began the attack on Tobruk, 4 RHA taking part in the fire programme. The following day the brigade, taking 3rd Hussars also under command, advanced straight to Mechili, where the Italians' sole remaining mobile force was known to be. Owing to a combination of unfortunate circumstances, we failed to prevent their escape into the hilly country to the north. The only maps were extremely old and inaccurate Italian ones, the tanks were nearly empty of petrol and to make it worse a dust storm was raging when the brigade reached Mechili. While Derna was being captured by the Australians, a further pause ensued to allow the much harassed administrative services to catch up.

It now became clear that the Italians were intending to abandon Benghazi and evacuate Cyrenaica altogether. In spite of the great administrative risks involved, the division advanced south-west from Mechili on February 5th, the brigade leading. While the brigade was filling up at a dump formed 30 miles south-west of Mechili, news came that 208 (A/C) Squadron RAF had seen a great convoy moving south from Benghazi. A wheeled force was hurriedly formed consisting of 11th Hussars, 4 RHA, 2nd Battalion The Rifle Brigade and one battery of 106 Anti-Tank Regiment RHA. This preceded the brigade, heading straight for the coast road west of Msus. As soon as replenishment was complete, the brigade set off again, having to traverse fifteen miles of the worst stony ground ever experienced. The delay was exasperating: to make up for it the brigade carried on until the moon went down at one o'clock in the morning of February 6th, by which time the brigade was some ten miles east of Msus.

Petrol was again the deciding factor. A third line RASC company full of petrol had been brought on from the dump without authority and had got lost during the hectic night march. By midday however petrol had been scraped up by robbing everyone else, and the brigade was able to start again, heading straight for Antelat, Sceleidima being held by the enemy. Late that night Colonel John Combe's wheeled force had cut the road, arriving two hours ahead of the Italians. Throughout February 7th the Rifle Brigade held the road while 4 RHA pounded away precious ammunition at the bewildered Italians. By the evening 4th Armoured Brigade, considerably depleted as a result of mechanical troubles, had reached the cross tracks near two water pumps known as Beda Fomm. On the morning of February 8th the Italians made one more futile attempt to break through the Rifle Brigade on the coast road, while the brigade, destroying a detachment of Italian tanks trying to outflank the Rifle Brigade on the east on its way, swung up to the road and raked with fire the mass of tanks, lorries and vehicles of all descriptions trapped between 2 RB and 4 RHA in the south and 1 KRRC in the north. It was not long before all was over and the last remnants of Graziani's army surrendered.

Tens of thousands of prisoners had been taken in this lightning campaign and a whole army destroyed at the cost of very few casualties on our side. Mechanically however we were exhausted. The whole division could only muster twelve cruisers and forty light tanks fit for another hundred miles. Bedecked with flags the brigade returned triumphant to Cairo, which it reached on February 23rd 1941, leaving all its tanks behind. There it began to reequip slowly with tanks repaired in the base workshops, celebrating its victory with the Christmas fare which had never been able to catch it up.

CHAPTER II

TOBRUK

Relief and Loss — May 1941 to July 1942

At the beginning of April 1941 Brigadier Caunter left the brigade to go to India: he was succeeded by Brigadier A. H. Gatehouse, DSO, MC. At the same time Rommel counter attacked at Agheila, and was soon at the gates of Tobruk. 11th Hussars and the Support Group were rushed up to hold the frontier. The brigade had no tanks and was forced to stay in Cairo. In May an unsuccessful attempt to relieve Tobruk had resulted in the recapture of Halfaya and Capuzzo, both of which were lost again when Rommel counterattacked on May 30th. A major operation to relieve Tobruk, called Operation Battleaxe, was planned for the middle of June: for this operation the brigade took over command of 4th Royal Tanks and 7th Royal Tanks, the latter having one squadron of 1st Royal Tanks under command, both equipped with Matildas.

We were to advance on the left flank of 4th Indian Division along the top of the escarpment towards Halfaya, while the rest of 7th Armoured Division were to outflank Capuzzo from the south. The battle opened on June 15th and lasted till the 21st. It was a complete failure. The unreliable, painfully slow Matildas were never designed to operate as cruiser tanks. Many broke down on their way to their objectives: many more were knocked out by 88s before they knew what had hit them. On our left 7th Armoured Brigade were having an equally bad time against German Mark IIIs and 88s, 6th Royal Tanks in particular suffering heavy losses at Hafid Ridge. The attack was a complete failure and was only saved from turning to disaster by the brilliant work of 4 RHA under the command of Jock Campbell, their 25 pounders being the only guns we had which could compete with the German tanks. In this battle the brigade lost almost all its tanks and 4th and 7th Royal Tanks were withdrawn to Alexandria, where they were joined by their original brigade HQ, 1st Army Tank Brigade, arrived from England.

4th Armoured Brigade HQ returned to Cairo to form a new brigade. As armoured regiments we now had 8th Hussars from 7th Armoured Brigade, 3rd Royal Tanks returned from Greece where they had served with 1st Armoured Brigade, and 5th Royal Tanks, survivors of the illfated 3rd Armoured Brigade, lost in Cyrenaica in April. In addition we were joined by 2nd Regiment Royal Horse Artillery, also from 1st Armoured Brigade, and as our motor battalion we welcomed 2nd Battalion Scots Guards. We were thus the first armoured brigade group ever to be formed.

In September we returned to the desert and continued training near Bir Kenayis, south-west of Matruh, moving up to join the rest of the division at the end of October between Piccadilly and Maddalena.

During the summer many changes had taken place. General 'Strafer' Gott had succeeded General Creagh in command of 7th Armoured Division and Jock Campbell had taken his place in command of the Support Group, John Currie succeeding him in command of 4 RHA. Eighth Army had been formed, General Cunningham being appointed to command. In October we were joined by 22nd Armoured Brigade, consisting of the 3rd and 4th County of London Yeomanry (Sharpshooters) and the 2nd Royal Gloucestershire Hussars. They had come ahead of the rest of 1st Armoured Division and were equipped entirely with the new Crusader tanks (A 15).

Before dawn on November 18th we crossed the frontier once again, the beginning of Operation "Crusader". After passing through the wire, we turned north and at Bir Sciafsciuf had our first brush with the enemy. This proved indecisive, the enemy withdrawing during the night. Advancing north the following morning we met the whole of 15th Panzer Division at Gabr Taieb el Essem, north-west of Scheferzen. A fierce battle ensued, in which we did our best to overcome the disadvantages of armour and armament, but suffered heavily as a result, 8th Hussars having particularly heavy casualties. The battle continued in the same area on the 20th, the enemy being reinforced by 21 Panzer Division at the end of the day. Meanwhile 22nd Armoured Brigade had been ordered to move east from Bir Gobi to join us. During the night 20/21st the enemy moved west: we made contact with him at Gabr Saleh early in the morning of the 21st, being joined later there by 22nd Armoured Brigade. Another fierce battle followed until the enemy began to withdraw north-west towards Sidi Rezegh, where 7th Armoured Brigade and Support Group were holding the aerodrome. We pursued as far as we could but, owing to our short range, had to stop and refuel. We caught up again on the 22nd and helped to relieve pressure on 7th Armoured Brigade and Support Group, who had been facing alone the combined onslaught of 15th and 21st Panzer and 90th Light Divisions.

On the 23rd the initiative definitely passed to the enemy. 5th South African Brigade, protected by the remnants of 22nd Armoured Brigade, were completely overrun at the cost to the Germans of 45 tanks. Support Group had suffered heavy casualties and 7th Armoured Brigade with it was reduced to less than a squadron of tanks. Support Group and 7th Armoured Brigade therefore were withdrawn on the night of 23/24th, 4th Armoured Brigade remaining in the area east of Sidi Rezegh to protect the left flank of 2 NZ Division, who had come west from Sidi Azeiz, by-passing Capuzzo. On the 24th Rommel advanced east from Bir Gobi, along the Trigh el Abd, and south-east from Sidi Rezegh. His advance passed north of 1st South African Brigade, south of most of 7th Armoured Division, through the north edge of 30 Corps FMC and drove 30 Corps Headquarters before it all the way to Scheferzen. It caused considerable confusion but surprisingly little damage.

During the night Support Group and Div HQ drove through the enemy from north to south and settled down to protect the FMC. The combined strength of 4 and 22 Armoured Brigades on this day, November 25th, was about 50 mixed Crusaders and Stuarts. 7th Armoured Brigade had ceased to exist. All the tanks were therefore concentrated in 4th Armoured Brigade which moved to Bir Taieb el Essem, on the Trigh el Abd between Bir Gobi and Gabr Saleh, to protect 1st South African Brigade who were being menaced by a party of tanks which Rommel had left behind.

On the 26th the terrific efforts of workshops and recovery produced more tanks, and the brigades split again, 4th having 77 Stuarts and 22nd 42 Crusaders. On the 27th Rommel, having achieved nothing by his wild drive across the desert to join hands with his frontier outposts, still holding out, began to move north to Sidi Azeiz and thence west along the Trigh Capuzzo, heading for Sidi Rezegh again. The brigade, with 22nd Armoured Brigade, was ordered north to intercept him and made contact near Gasr el Arid at two o'clock in the afternoon, Support Group meanwhile harrying the tail of the column to the east.

Throughout 28th and 29th we continued a running battle on the Trigh Capuzzo near Bir Chleta, trying to prevent Rommel joining hands with Rawenstein and thus cutting off the New Zealand Division, which had linked up with the garrison of Tobruk at Belhamed. It became more and more difficult, pressure on the New Zealanders from the west increasing daily. On the 30th 1st South African Brigade moved north east from Bir Taieb el Essem to the escarpment east of Sidi Rezegh, while we protected their right flank. During that night they tried to drive west along the escarpment to join hands with the New Zealanders at Sidi Rezegh, but they could not get beyond a hill called Pt 175 to the east of the aerodrome. At first light on December 1st they were astride the escarpment, Support Group on their right flank, east of the New Zealand Division, ourselves on their left flank at Abiar el Nbeidat.

General Freyberg was now being attacked from north and south, had little ammunition left and had been given permission to withdraw by General Norrie, who had made contact with him and under whose command he had now been placed, communications with 13 Corps in Tobruk having been cut again. In order to cover the withdrawal of the New Zealand Div and to try and save the many already surrounded, 4th Armoured Brigade were ordered to drive straight down to Belhamed, across Sidi Rezegh aerodrome, between the enemy on the escarpments on either side. At eight o'clock we advanced into a situation resembling in almost every detail the charge of the light brigade at Balaclava. We reached Belhamed, rallied and protected a brigade of the New Zealand Division which had been partially overrun and held off all counter-attacks, until the New Zealanders had withdrawn to the east and re-organized. We then returned to our station on the south flank of 1st South African Brigade.

Tobruk was now entirely cut off again. The brigade, with the rest of the division, was withdrawn to the Trigh el Abd in preparation for a thrust in co-operation with 4th Indian Division towards El Adem. After one more attempt to get supplies to his immobile troops sitting in the defences at Halfaya and Bardia, the enemy concentrated his forces between Bir Gobi and El Adem. From December 4th to 6th 11 Indian Brigade attacked the enemy position at Bir Gobi. Every attempt to outflank it made by the brigade was invariably met by a screen of anti-tank guns, backed up by tanks. Operating on the inside of the circle, the enemy could and did forestall us every time. On December 7th the enemy began to withdraw north-west and contact was again made with 70th Division in Tobruk. We had a successful last light battle between El Adem and Bir Acroma on that day: by the following morning the enemy had withdrawn completely clear of Tobruk perimeter. 22nd Amoured Brigade was now withdrawn, leaving us, the only armoured brigade still in the division, with a composite regiment made up from their three regiments.

The brigade was now launched on a wide outflanking movement, designed to cut off the enemy in the area of Bir Temrad. After a savage counter-attack against 5th Indian

Brigade, the enemy withdrew rapidly as the threat developed. We pursued to Mechili and then lost touch. Following our old tracks, we continued the pursuit to Msus and Agedabia, where we were relieved by 1st Armoured Division.

Rommel had started the battle with nearly 300 tanks, excluding Italian. We had started with a superiority of 3 to 2 in numbers, but, except in the case of the Italians, we were in every case inferior in armament and armour. The crusaders and Matildas of 22nd and 1st Army Tank Brigades respectively were also extremely unreliable. The enemy's most outstanding superiority was in anti-tank guns. The South African Division had a few 18 pounders: apart from them the two-pounder was the best we had and they were not in liberal supply. In spite of these disadvantages we had driven the enemy from the frontier of Egypt and the perimeter of Tobruk out of Cyrenaica altogether, reducing him, until reinforcements reached Benghazi by sea, to a strength of 8 tanks at one time. Let nobody ever belittle the remarkable achivements of the Crusader operation. That the fruits of our success were so soon to be lost again in our absence was as bitter a disappointment as it had been the year before.

We returned again exhausted and somewhat disorganized to Cairo. We reformed again with the same armoured regiments, 1st RHA, released from Tobruk, replacing 2 RHA, and 1st Battalion KRRC from the Support Group replacing 2nd Battalion Scots Guards. We were equipped again with Stuarts and, as they became available, with Grants. In them at last we felt we had a tank, which if not the superior, was at least able to take on a German tank on more or less equal terms.

In April we returned to the desert and continued training south of Sidi Azeiz. Brigadier Gatehouse, who had commanded the brigade with skill and vigour through many difficult and anxious battles, now left us to take over command of 10th Armoured Division. In his place Brigadier G. W. Richards, DSO, MC came to us, having been GSO 1 of 7th Armoured Division throughout the Crusader operation and then second-in-command of 22nd Armoured Brigade. At the beginning of May we moved up to the area east of Bir Hacheim, relieving 1st Armoured Division. By now each armoured regiment had 24 Grants and 20 Stuarts, and 1 RHA's anti-tank battery was being equipped with the new 6-pounder guns. We continued training, concentrating particularly on gunnery and artillery support. Plans were afoot for an offensive, an operation to be called Buckshot designed to recapture Benghazi; but it soon became clear that Rommel was intending to attack shortly too, and it was decided to let him run his head into the trap.

On May 26th a large column moved east from Segnali, apparently heading straight down the Trigh Capuzzo. Before last light part of the column was seen to turn south-east. During the night the whole force, joined by others moving direct from Segnali, turned south and by first light had refuelled south of Bir Hacheim. At 5 o'clock in the morning the brigade received the order to move to its southern battle position. At eight o'clock we found ourselves faced by the whole of 15 and 21 Panzer Divisions, with one regiment still not in position. A fierce battle ensued in which we lost almost all our tanks. 90th Light Division had meanwhile swept past us to the east and reached the outskirts of El Adem. Divisional HQ had been overrun and had ceased to exist. 22nd Armoured Brigade, caught facing the wrong way by a battle group which had overrun 3rd Indian Motor Brigade and passed between us and Hacheim, had suffered heavily. The French were firm in Hacheim, having repulsed Ariete Division:

the Guards were firm as a rock in Knightsbridge. 2nd Armoured Brigade were more or less intact south-west of El Adem. By the end of the day the remnants of the brigade had rallied and were holding the escarpment east of the El Adem box, after as disastrous a day as the brigade has ever known.

The enemy was as disorganized as we: he tried to reach Acroma, failed, and then collected himself in the Cauldron, breaking out of it westwards to re-establish his L of C, overrunning 151 Brigade and 1 Army Tank Brigade in so doing. In an attempt to destroy him in the cauldron and relieve pressure on 151 Brigade, an attack was put in from the east in which 4th Armoured Brigade did not take part. It was a failure and cost 1st Armoured Division and 10th Indian Division heavy casualties. By now all armoured brigades were much depleted and disorganized. 1st Armoured Brigade, brought up to Capuzzo, was split up and distributed among the other brigades. Regiments were amalgamated and reformed every day. Brigades changed regiments and divisions changed brigades, sometimes more than once a day. By June 11th, the day after the withdrawal from Hacheim, the remains of four armoured brigades, 1st, 2nd, 4th and 22nd, were all under command of 4th Armoured Brigade in the area between El Adem and Knightsbridge. During the 12th the enemy moved in groups eastwards from the minefield near Bir Harmat to the Wadi running south-west from El Adem, near Hagfet Sciaaban. By the end of the day he had concentrated all his armoured strength in this area behind us and directly threatening El Adem, Belhamed and the gateway to Tobruk. During the night he dug in his anti-tank guns on the lip of the wadi. On the morning of June 13th we were ordered to advance south from our battle position, around the withered fig tree of Naduret el Ghesceuasc, to engage the enemy concentration. Using hardly any of his tanks, but almost entirely with his anti-tank guns, the enemy reduced the brigade to a handful of tanks. Up till then his losses in tanks had generally been in the same proportion to his total strength as our own. By the end of the 13th we had lost almost all we had left and he none at all. The die was cast: the initiative was now his, with Tobruk and Belhamed crammed with unnecessary stores and L of C troops, put there for the projected offensive, with 50 Div and the South Africans still strung out well to the west of Tobruk. It was a grim prospect. That night the gallant Guards Brigade, who had clung so grimly to Knightsbridge, were withdrawn, 2nd Armoured Brigade taking command of all tanks west of El Adem, while we took over all the tanks east of it, which included the daily flow of motley tanks and crews formed from stragglers and recovered and repaired tanks. While Tobruk was defended and lost and the whole army withdrew eastwards, the brigade daily fought delaying actions against Rommel's 15th and 21st Panzer Divisions, who strove in vain to cut off the columns retreating along the coast. Daily our strength fell: sleep was as precious as it was rare. When we reached the Matruh-Siwa road, we were relieved by 1st Armoured Division and handed over to them the mixed collection of regiments and tanks we still had left.

CHAPTER III

Fourth light — Alamein to Tunis — July 1942 to May 1943

In order to watch the wide left flank of the Alamein — Himeimat line and to control the increasing number of armoured car regiments becoming available, 4th Armoured Brigade was now reformed as a Light Armoured Brigade. Brigadier W. G. Carr, DSO, then commanding 22nd Armoured Brigade, a 12th Lancer who had commanded 4th CLY, took over command from Brigadier Richards. The task of patrolling on sectors on which contact was slight had in the past generally been done by the support group, later the motor brigade of the division. The disadvantages of tying the motor brigade down to this task had been made painfully clear in May. Although officially now an independent brigade, we continued to serve under command of 7th Armoured Division and to carry their sign. 22nd Armoured Brigade took our place as the armoured brigade of the division, a place it has filled ever since. At first the brigade was composed of 11th Hussars and 12th Lancers, 4th Hussars with one squadron of 8th Hussars, equipped entirely with Stuarts, RHQ and one squadron of 3rd CLY (Sharpshooters) 3 RHA and 1st Bn KRRC. After 69 Brigade's abortive attack on the Taqa plateau, we took our place on the left of the line, 1 KRRC, supported by 4/8 Hussars holding Himeimat, with one company back at Samaket Gaballa with the Sharpshooters. 11th Hussars and 12th Lancers took it in turns to patrol south of the escarpment to Maghra, and to send long distance patrols as far afield as Qara. There was little incident until, on the last night of August, Rommel made his final attack to reach Alexandria. Breaking through the minefield north of Himeimat, he advanced slowly, picking his way as cautiously through dummy as through real minefields, to Deir el Ragil, harassed by the brigade on his right and rear. His advance however had forced us to abandon first Himeimat and then Samaket Gaballa, as it had always been foreseen that it would. When he turned north east on the following day, we continued to harry his long right flank as his head came to an abrupt halt, held by 22nd and 8th Armoured Brigades. After several days' battering from the ground and air, he withdrew to a line running north from Himeimat, to which he clung. We continued to carry on with our old job.

The formation of 10 Corps wrought many changes. Brigadier Carr went home, replaced by Brigadier Mark Roddick, recently arrived from England as second in command of 22nd Armoured Brigade. 12th Lancers left us, replaced by 2nd Derbyshire Yeomanry, and we were reinforced by The Royal Scots Greys, who had been serving as a fourth regiment in 22nd Armoured Brigade, after coming into the field ahead of the rest of their original armoured Brigade, the 8th. The Sharpshooters left us to reform in the Delta.

Shortly before the battle of Alamein, we were relieved by 1st Free French Brigade, and lost the Greys to 22nd Armoured Brigade. We carried out several exercises to practise our future role of exploiting the break-through, even to the extent of being equipped with carrier-pigeons. When the battle of Alamein began on October 23rd, we were in reserve under 7th

Armoured Division, ready to pass through 22nd Armoured Brigade, if they succeeded in breaking through the minefields east of Gebel Kalakh. This they had not managed to do when they were withdrawn from the south and sent up north on November 1st. The Greys rejoined us, but 11th Hussars left with 7th Armoured Division, 1st Household Cavalry Regiment taking their place. By November 4th the enemy had been finally broken, and 1st and 7th Armoured Divisions had begun to break out. The Brigade, under command of 2nd New Zealand Division passed through on the left, heading straight for the escarpment west of Fuka. We reached this, after capturing crowds of prisoners, on the afternoon of the 5th, but were held up there by a determined rearguard of 15th Panzer Division. 7th Armoured Division that night crossed us and turned north on our left. A short pause for petrol followed, while it poured with rain: we then continued the advance along the coast road west from Matruh, while 7th Armoured Division drove west well into the desert to the south. Late on the 11th, after dealing with a series of rearguards, we reached the foot of Halfaya Pass defended by the Italian Pistoia Division reinforced by Germans. This was attacked by the New Zealanders during the night: first light found us at the head of the pass in time to join hands with 22nd Armoured Brigade coming from the south. The enemy made no attempt to hold Bardia which we entered that afternoon.

    We now returned to 7th Armoured Division, taking over command of the Royals and 4th South African Armoured Car Regiment in place of 2 Derby Yeo and the Household Cavalry. Taking a wide sweep to the south, we reached Knightsbridge at last light on the 13th and Acroma on the morning of the 14th, capturing the tail of the Germans fleeing west from Tobruk. Leaving the Royals under command of 7th Armoured Division, and also leaving behind 4/8th Hussars, who handed over their few remaining tanks to the Greys, we continued the pursuit along the coast road into the Gebel.

    Mines and road blocks were our trouble here and progress was slower. Brigadier Roddick was himself wounded on a mine and was succeeded by Brigadier C. B. (Roscoe) Harvey, DSO, another 10th Hussar. We entered Benghazi on November 20th, just beating the 11th Hussars, who came from the south.

    We paused there for a few days while the King's Dragoon Guards took the place of 4th South African Armoured Car Regiment. We then rejoined the rest of 7th Armoured Division between Agedabia and Agheila, and took up our usual position on the open left flank, the Royals returning to our command.

    By 25th November Rommel had managed to form a firm defensive position at Mersa Brega, which could not be assaulted or turned by the slender forces which were all we had there and could maintain at the time. By December 12th 30 Corps had taken over control over operations from 10 Corps, bringing up 51st (Highland) Division and the 2nd New Zealand Division. 8th Armoured Brigade had replaced 22nd Armoured Brigade in 7th Armoured Division and we passed to the command of the New Zealand Division on the left flank, prepared to outflank the Mersa Brega — Agheila position by a direct advance north of Marada to cut the road between Agheila and Marble Arch. Faced with this threat, the enemy began to withdraw: by that time we were south-west of Agheila, but had not cut the coast road to the north. On the 15th December, while we protected the left flank, New Zealand troops turned north to do this, but got into great difficulties in trying to cross a very large soft wadi.

The main body of the enemy got away to the west that night by the light of a brilliant moon. During the 16th we had a running fight all day with a succession of rearguards, and on the morning of the 17th met the enemy's main body near Nofilia. The Greys closed in on the village from the east and south while the KDG watched the west. The leading squadron of the Greys overran the enemy's forward positions, capturing some 200 prisoners. A tank battle followed against some 30 German tanks, while the New Zealand Division passed round to the south of us in an attempt to outflank Nofilia and cut the road north-west of where the battle was going on. The enemy recognized the threat and began to withdraw, aided by the oncoming darkness. During the night the whole force withdrew. 7th Armoured Division now took on the pursuit and we stayed near Nofilia. 1st Bn KRRC left us to join 7 Motor Brigade, being very much in need of rest and re-equipment. Their place was taken by the 2nd Battalion, who have stayed with us ever since.

On the 21st we rejoined 7th Armoured Division, leaving the Greys behind with the New Zealand Division, with whom they were to stay for the rest of the campaign in North Africa. By the 24th we had closed up to the rearguard position just east of Sirte, which was evacuated that night. A thick ground mist and the presence of many mines and booby traps around Sirte delayed the pursuit, and it was not until Boxing Day that we regained contact with a rearguard of some strength on the Wadi Chebir. This rearguard withdrew on the night of the 27th into the enemy's main position, which was found to run from the sea just north of Buerat el Hsun, south-west across the main road west of the village, thence parallel to and south of the road to about 5 miles south-east of Gheddahia, whence patrols operated southwards along the line of the track to Bu Ngem. We took over the task of observation and keeping contact with the enemy along the entire front, 11th Hussars also coming under our command.

A further pause followed while supplies were built up, landing grounds built and more troops brought forward. Our main trouble in these weeks came from the GAF who carried out a daily strafe of our area. Patrols of SAS and LRDG were busy at this time spying out the land behind the enemy's line in preparation for our next move.

On the morning of January 15th, 8th Armoured Brigade crossed the road from Gheddahia to Bu Ngem, the New Zealand Division coming up on their left. We crossed the New Zealand Division to our traditional station on the open left flank, remaining under command of 7th Armoured Division, although the New Zealand Division was between us and the rest of the division. Our objective was Beni Ulid and our route a narrow defile through the broken desert, previously reconnoitred by the LRDG. It was atrocious going and progress slow. It was not till the afternoon of the 17th that we made contact with the enemy east of Beni Ulid, which 8th Amoured Brigade were beginning to outflank from the north-east. Enemy vehicles were closely packed in the village: in the failing light 2nd Bn KRRC, supported by 3rd RHA, closed up on the tail of the column and caused much damage, continuing to shoot it up after dark. The enemy got away what he could during the night, but when we entered the village in the morning we collected a fair haul of prisoners and found a large number of destroyed or abandoned vehicles including thirteen Italian M 13 tanks. We could not continue up the main road to Tarhuna as the bridge was blown and there was no possible deviation. We set off therefore by a very indifferent track west of the main road, hoping to reach the track from Tarhuna to Garian about half way between the two. Every arab assured us that the country was impassable, to all but donkeys and camels. It was not impassable, but it was the nearest thing to it imaginable. To add to the trials imposed by the frightful difficulties of the rocky, hilly country intersected by sheer wadis, we were subject to continuous attacks by Stukas and Messerschmitts. However we struggled through somehow and were rewarded by KDG finding what everyone was looking for, a way down the escarpment west of Tarhuna. On January 20th KDG went down the escarpment into the sea of soft sand below, while the Royals turned west along the track to Garian. KDG met some German tanks south of Azizia which might have proved troublesome, as their armoured cars were all getting stuck. On the 21st the rest of the brigade, less the Royals and one battery of 3rd RHA, who had met an enemy rearguard east of Garian, descended the escarpment, the Greys leading the New Zealand Division following us and coming up on our right. While others raced for Tripoli, we turned west above and below the escarpment.

On the 22nd the Royals entered Garian, welcomed by the Italians as protection against the Arabs: there they joined hands the following day with General Leclerc's Free French force, which had come all the way from Lake Chad. While the rest of the division was celebrating the capture of Tripoli, we pushed further west to Jefren, communication with the Royals being made difficult by the fact that the roads up the escarpment at Garian and Jefren were both blown. 4th Field Squadron RE mended the blow below Jefren and we were able to join forces again. Extended to our utmost limit we pushed further westwards, and on February 2nd crossed the frontier into Tunisia, the first troops of Eighth Army to do so. Here we were up against old enemies, the German 3rd and 33rd Reconnaissance units, and continued to have very considerable trouble from the Luftwaffe.

At the end of January Brigadier Harvey left us to take over command of 8th Armoured Brigade: he was succeeded by Brigadier D. S. Newton King, DSO, who had for so long commanded the 4th South African Armoured Car Regiment and had more recently been second-in-command of 22nd Armoured Brigade.

Gradually we forced back the enemy's patrols to a close ring round Foum Tatahouine. The rest of the division meanwhile was struggling with the salt marshes near El Assa: after a causeway had been built, Ben Gardane was captured on February 15th, and 12th Lancers quickly closed up to Medenine. Meanwhile we faced the problem of capturing Foum Tatahouine, a hilly stronghold on the edge of the ridge of mountains running south-east from the Mareth Line. By a brilliantly conducted attack 2nd Bn KRRC captured the key position commanding the approach from the east and quickly cleared the village itself. We now began pushing up the narrow tracks into the mountains, and linked up with the rest of the division on our right south of Medenine. As we pushed the enemy back northwards, we opened up a route through the mountains and joined hands again with General Leclerc on the far side. Brigadier Newton King was now succeeded by Brigadier John Currie, DSO, MC. At Alamein he had commanded 9th Armoured Brigade, before which he had commanded 2nd Armoured Brigade for a short time. At the beginning of March the Free French Flying Column, a small party of mobile troops which included a squadron of Crusader tanks, came under our command.

The New Zealand Division, with the Greys still under their command, also arrived to take over the area of Medenine and we came under them. On March 6th Rommel made his famous attack on Metameur and Medenine from the west. One colunm struck south-east and was hotly engaged by the Free French Flying Column. By the end of the day it had been driven back to join the main body in its rout. After the battle we continued our difficult and novel task of mountain warfare. A Ghurka battalion came under our command from 4th Indian Division and soon made the mountains unpopular with the enemy. Before the Battle of Mareth began, the New Zealand Division with the Greys passed through us, by the mountain route we had opened up, to join General Leclerc west of the hills, and we came under command of 1st Armoured Division who had taken their place.

The Battle of Mareth opened on March 21st. On the 24th, when it was clear that the 50th Division's attack at the north end of the line had failed, 1st Armoured Division crossed the mountains to join the New Zealand Division south of El Hamma and 4th Indian Division took on the job of clearing the mountains. We returned to 7th Armoured Division moving up to the area west of Medenine between 22nd Armoured Brigade and 4th Indian Division. Our final job in the Battle of Mareth was the capture of the precipitous foothills astride the main road to Toujane, which was brilliantly carried out by 2nd Bn KRRC; their attack, and that of 1st Bn The Rifle Brigade on their right, resulting in the capture of a large part of the Italian Pistoia Division. Meanwhile the New Zealand Division, with their faithful Royal Scots Greys, and 1st Armoured Division had inflicted a crushing defeat on the enemy at El Hamma and forced him back to the line of the Wadi Akarit. We moved up to near Gabes with 7th Armoured Division, but left them there to join 10 Corps. We took no part in the battle of Akarit itself, which opened on April 6th, but followed 1st Armoured Division through and came out on their left, watching the open flank between them and the American 1st Armoured Division of First Army. We continued this task without incident as 1st Armoured Division advanced to La Fauconerie and Kairouan. At Kairouan we relieved 1st Armoured Division, who went to join First Army, and found ourselves between General Leclerc's Free French force on our right and the 19th French Corps of General Giraud's forces on our left, a tricky situation. We continued the advance north capturing Djebibina and pushing the enemy back into the foothills to the north. It was an unpleasant position in open low ground, overlooked by mountains on all sides: enemy shelling was intense and accurate, causing many casualties. We took command of General Leclerc's force, coming under command of 7th Armoured Division later, when they moved up to Kairouan on April 16th. Between April 20th and 27th we pushed the enemy further back still into the hills, 22nd Armoured Brigade coming up on our right near Djebel Fadeloun, while New Zealand Division were attacking Enfidaville and Takruna and 4th Indian Division scaling Djebel Garci. On the 28th 7th Armoured Division and 4th Indian Division were taken away to go round to First Army, and all further ideas of an attack on Eighth Army's front were abandoned. We returned to the command of the New Zealand Division. Our only other moment of excitement between then and the end of the campaign in North Africa on May 13th, was the negotiation of the surrender of the Italian Army by General Messe to General Freyberg. The operator on the brigade command net picked up a message from General Messe, which was passed to General Freyberg. We arranged a rendezvous for their representatives by the same means. We were sorry not to be in on the triumphant entry into Tunis, but could feel that we had contributed a very fair share to victory in North Africa since our formation in Egypt three and a half years before.

CHAPTER IV

Sicily, Italy and Home — June 1943 to June 1944

With the end of the North African campaign, Fourth Light was wound up and the brigade reformed as a normal armoured brigade, less one regiment to begin with. 3 RHA left us to join 7th Armoured Division, 2 KRRC settled down near Tripoli temporarily under command of 1st Armoured Division: The Royals became Corps troops of 13 Corps, KDG of 10 Corps. Brigade HQ left Sfax on May 21st to return to the Delta of Egypt for the last time reaching Beni Yusef on June 4th, coming under 13 Corps. June 1st was the official date when "Light" was dropped from our title. Our two new regiments were 3rd County of London Yeomanry (Sharpshooters) and 44th Royal Tanks. 3 CLY had been part of the original 22nd Armoured Brigade and had been reforming in Egypt since before Alamein. 44th Royal Tanks had come to the Middle East in the summer of 1941 and had first seen battle under 1st Army Tank Brigade in the Crusader operation. They had played a notable part in the fighting round Belhamed and Sidi Rezegh and later in the capture of Bardia by 2nd South African Division. In the Knightsbridge battle they were part of the ill-fated 1st Army Tank Brigade which suffered heavily with 151 Brigade. Reformed, they took part in the withdrawal to Alamein and in the battles round Alamein itself in June and July 1942. In the Battle of Alamein itself they had been equipped with flail mine-clearing tanks, the first regiment ever to be equipped with them.

Both regiments were now fully up to strength and equipped with Diesel Shermans. Never had the brigade been so well and thoroughly equipped.

13 Corps' planning for the invasion of Sicily was already far advanced: 3 CLY had already been placed under command of the 5th Division and 44th Royal Tanks under the 50th (Northumbrian) Division. Tactical Brigade HQ was to accompany HQ 13 Corps for the invasion, the rest of the headquarters following on D + 28. 2 KRRC were to remain at Tripoli. During June the regiments were loaded, distributed over a large variety of craft, Tac Brigade being at Port Said on board HMS Bulolo and LSP Dilwara. On July 5th we sailed from Port Said: after an uneventful voyage we arrived off the Sicilian coast on the night of 9/10th July. Brigade HQ was not controlling the two regiments and their stories must be given separately up to the 21st.

The Sharpshooters with 5th Division were due to land shortly after first light. It was not however till midday that the first tanks, half of C squadron, supporting 13 Infantry Brigade, came ashore. At 3 o'clock nine tanks of B Squadron also landed: they joined 17 Infantry Brigade beyond Cassibile in the late afternoon and entered Syracuse at last light. C Squadron meanwhile had had a small evening battle south of Florida. On the 11th the rest of the regiment landed, B Squadron meanwhile carrying on the advance north of Syracuse with 2nd Bn Northamptons. A party of enemy in the woods south of Priolo held up this advance all day and movement off the road was very difficult: in trying to move down the road three tanks were knocked out. A Squadron meanwhile sent a troop into Syracuse to help in the final clearing of the town. The half of C Squadron that was with 13 Brigade had entered Florida at eight after a short engagement: they continued the advance towards Taverna and had quite a battle to capture Solarino. For the loss of two tanks they destroyed one French R 35 tank and several guns and mortars. They were joined at Taverna by the rest of the squadron which had landed in the afternoon.

On the 12th B Squadron with 17 Brigade entered Priolo at half past eight, but were held up on the river to the north where the bridge was held. The river was a considerable obstacle, and it was only after an attack with two battalions that tanks were able to cross. Just before last light, after several unsuccessful attempts, two tanks got over and supported 6th Bn Seaforths into Augusta during the night. On the 13th A Squadron relieved C Squadron with 13 Brigade, and continued the advance until the enemy were met at five in the afternoon north of Tentilla. An attack was put in, in which half of the squadron took part: the enemy counter-attacked strongly with tanks: six of the seven Sharpshooter tanks were knocked out. No further advance took place that day and the regiment was concentrated north of Priolo.

At six o-clock in the evening of July 10th half of A Squadron of 44th Royal Tanks had landed with 50th Division, followed four hours later by the rest of the squadron. The following day the rest of the regiment landed, less 9 tanks of C Squadron which were lost when their ship sank before landing. The regiment concentrated east of Avola, moving on the 12th to east of Florida, less A Squadron which led the advance of 69 Brigade through Palazzolo, directed on Solarino. They met the enemy beyond Palazzolo and destroyed four guns, took sixty prisoners and killed many more. A further attempt to advance met strong opposition towards last light. After dark the advance was called off and the squadron withdrawn to Cancattini Bagni. On the 13th C Squadron, weak having lost 9 tanks at sea, was placed under command of 151 Brigade to clear the enemy still between Palazzolo, now held by the Highland Division, and Solarino. A mobile column from the brigade, led by a troop of C Squadron, was first held up by a burning lorry: the leading tank charged straight through it to clear the way for carriers to resume the lead. Round the next corner a R 35 tank engaged the first carrier: from then on the tanks went into the lead. The leading tank was fired on by ten R 35s and in reply knocked out two R 35s, 4 cars and 3 lorries. This blocked the road completely. Looking on foot for a way round, the troop leader saw a white flag and, on going up to it, received the surrender of the commander and staff of the Italian 54th Napoli Division. Continuing the advance, an antitank gun and some 105 mms were met: with the help of a company of 6th DLI they destroyed 4 guns, 11 lorries and 3 more R 35s. Further on they met and destroyed 12 vehicles, 3 R 35s and a motor-cycle, bringing their total for the day to 8 tanks, 6 guns, 29 assorted vehicles and 3 motor-cycles, a great effort for one troop. The rest of the regiment had been concentrated. 50th Division's advance towards Lentini through the hills past Sortino was going well, but it was not thought possible to get tanks through by that route. Meanwhile the Corps Commander had decided to concentrate the brigade and use it to continue the advance to Catania, through Lentini. Accordingly the brigade, consisting of The Sharpshooters, 44th Royal Tanks and A Squadron of The Royals concentrated south of Priolo. 5th Division was no longer in contact with the enemy and we were told to move through Augusta to Villasmundo. To ensure that our route was clear half a squadron of Sharpshooters and a company of embussed infantry with carriers were to go as far as Villasmundo in the moonlight. There was considerable delay in getting this party married up and it was half past five in the morning of the 14th before they reported Villasmundo clear. The Sharpshooters led and passed through the town at eight o'clock. 50th Division were reported near Carlentini on the high ground to the south and we were placed under their command.

At 9 o'clock a persistent stranger on the brigade forward control was spoken to by Brigadier Currie and turned out to be the Headquarters of the Brigade of 1st Airborne Division, who were to have been dropped during the night to capture Primosole bridge, south of Catania. We had heard that they had been dropped in the wrong place, but their brigade HQ and a handful of men held the bridge. Spasmodic conversations with them continued for an hour, after which we heard no more. Meanwhile the fight for Carlentini was going slowly: the Sharpshooters were having great difficulty with the going and progress was slow without the support of infantry or artillery, the latter being provided later by the voluntary help of 24th Field Regiment. Eventually they joined hands with troops of 50th Division. As there was only one road and that a very bad one, it was decided to pass 44th Royal Tanks through, the Sharpshooters having run short of ammunition. This took a long time as tanks were continually shedding tracks on the rocky hairpin bends. In addition the move entailed overtaking troops and transport of 50th Division in the tortuous streets of Carlentini and Lentini. Eventually 44th Royal Tanks caught up with the leading troops of 69 Brigade: they were opposed by two German tanks and had met several small parties of our own airborne troops, none of whom however knew anything about Primosole bridge. One squadron of the 44th Royal Tanks was placed in support of 151 Brigade, but for various reasons the attack on the bridge was postponed until the following morning. The attack was launched early in the morning of the 15th supported by 44th Royal Tanks, while the Sharpshooters protected the left flank. Owing to mines and vehicles blocking the road, tanks could not cross the bridge: 151 Brigade had succeeded in making a very narrow bridgehead but were later withdrawn. Before dawn on the 16th a further attack was made: 8 DLI secured a bridgehead just large enough to allow the sappers to clear the mines and obstructions, which they did in time to let a squadron of the 44th Royal Tanks pass over at first light. Unfortunately the bridgehead was under accurate anti-tank fire and four tanks were knocked out, the CO and 3 other officers being killed. During the day the Royals had engaged many small parties of enemy on the bridges between the left of 50th Division and the right of 30 Corps, the Sharpshooters being concentrated in reserve. A further attack in the bridgehead area had been put in by 6 and 9 DLI during the night 16/17th. At first light the Sharpshooters, relieving 44th Royal Tanks with 151 Brigade, passed over the bridge. The bridgehead area continued to be most unhealthy, until the source of trouble, a strong point about 300 yards north-west of the bridge, was finally located and cleared by the Sharpshooters. Before that was done the Sharpshooters had lost their CO and 5 tank commanders from sniping. The battle for the bridge was now over and the Sharpshooters supported the extension of the bridgehead, being relieved by the 44th Royal Tanks on the 18th. During the day they had one sharp battle, assisting 1st Royal Berks who had been surrounded, and lost five tanks in doing so. On the 19th 13 Brigade of

5 Division passed through, supported by B Squadron of the 44th Royal Tanks, directed on Misterbianco. Little progress was made in the face of stiff opposition, a further five tanks being knocked out or damaged. On the 20th the Sharpshooters supported an attack by 5th Division to cross the River Simeto. For the rest of the month the brigade was in reserve. Of the 95 tanks with which we had landed, 25 had been knocked out. On July 22nd our tank strength was 67: it had never fallen below 55 in spite of practically no respite from movement or action, a great feat by the fitters.

On 1st August the advance was resumed against rearguards to Catania which was reached on the 5th, the brigade finally coming to rest at Aci Castello, a beautiful little seaside town eight miles to the north. 30 Corps now took over the advance up the coast and we came under their command. Our first task was to organize and command two seaborne expeditions to cut the coast road behind the enemy, one to land immediately behind the enemy line, within range of 50th Division's artillery, the other, known as operation Blackcock, to land an independent force near Cap D'Ali, the furthest north we could go without being troubled by coast defence guns on the Italian mainland. This force consisted of Tac Brigade HQ, No. 2 Commando, one squadron of the Sharpshooters, a troop of 56 Field Battery RA (SP), a troop of jeep-drawn 3.7 hows, a troop of 6 pounders and 295 Field Company RE less a platoon. The Commando were to sail in LSIs from Augusta, the rest embarking in LCTs at Catania. Within 48 hours the force had been collected east of Misterbianco, waterproofed and was ready to embark. Embarkation at Catania went very smoothly and the LCTs sailed punctually at eight in the evening of August 15th.

In the early part of the night the full moon became almost totally eclipsed, but was shining full again when we reached our rendezvous with the LSIs at two in the morning. We now saw the road at Cap D'Ali, our objective, being blown. It was decided therefore to land further north, although the beaches there had not ben reconnoitred. After some difficulty in finding exits from the beach, which was itself perfect, the force was landed at Cap Scaletta in broad daylight in face of accurate but intermittent shelling. We took up positions covering the road. No advance south to join 50th Division was possible as the road was blown in two places. The Brigadier therefore concentrated on advancing north towards Messina. As movement in daylight up the road was bound to be expensive, a moonlight advance was decided on. 2 Commando with the Sharpshooter squadron were to advance at eight and if possible continue to Messina. Demolitions and mines however caused considerable delay. At ten o'clock on the morning of the 17th we entered Messina to find the enemy had withdrawn over the ferry, leaving a vast heap of equipment behind. We met American patrols at the north end of the town and later General Patton himself was received in front of the town hall. Tac Brigade HQ and the squadron of Sharpshooters returned by road and sea to Riposto and back to Aci Castello.

46th and 50th Royal Tanks and 111 Field Regiment RA now came under our command from 23rd Armoured Brigade and we came into Army reserve.

On September 16th, orders were received for the brigade, less 111 Field Regiment RA, to move to Taranto: the Brigade Commander went in advance to report to 5 Corps to get the form. All tanks and tracked vehicles were to move by sea and the wheels by ferry from Messina, thence by road to Taranto. Brigade HQ arrived at Taranto on 23rd September and received orders to move to Bari area and come under command 78 Division, being prepared next day to take command of forward reconnaissance elements of the division.

Our force consisted of A Squadron The Royals, one squadron of the Sharpshooters, one squadron 56 Recce Regiment, recce squadron of 1 Air Landing Brigade, one company of 1 Kensingtons, 17 Field Regiment RA less one battery, SAS squadron and a similar body known as "Popski's Private Army". 626 Field Squadron RE joined the Force by bits and pieces and subsequently became part of the brigade.

This force had just captured Canosa and was meeting opposition across the River Ofanto, over which the bridge was blown: on the coast the town of Barletta was not yet occupied. Very little progress was made this day, but Barletta was finally entered and passed: 4th Armoured Brigade now became the spearhead of the Eighth Army in its advance up the east coast of Italy.

Once again our main opposition was enemy rearguards and demolitions. Enemy antitank guns were well placed and cleverly concealed. When a crossing over the River Ofanto had been found, the brigade moved very fast, until held up by defended demolitions on the line of the railway and the river south of Manfredonia. The Sharpshooters, who were working up the inland road, passed through Cerignola meeting no enemy until held up six miles south of Foggia. The fight went on until dark, when the enemy blew the bridges and withdrew. The advance was resumed at first light on the 27th: after struggling with demolitions, we entered Foggia, still burning from the Royal Air Force's attack the night before, to find much abandoned equipment. Meanwhile the Royals had found Manfredonia clear. San Severo was clear and 56 Recce Regiment entered Lucera, releasing many British and South African prisoners, survivors of Tobruk. Patrol bases were now established at San Severo, Lucera, Troia Satriano and San Paulo: for administrative reasons no major move forward could be undertaken before October 1st.

On this day the brigade was ordered to take the high ground on either side of Serracapriola and clear the way for 11 Infantry Brigade to advance to Termoli. For this operation 5th Northamptons came under our command. All bridges south of Serracapriola had been destroyed and there appeared to be only two possible crossings: one near the sea at Ripalto, the other about two miles upstream from the main road bridge. The Sharpshooters less a squadron were to cross by the latter and take the ridge south of the town: this done, 5th Northamptons were to cross nearer the main road, and attack Serracapriola through the thick olive groves round the town: meanwhile the Royals with one squadron of Sharpshooters and part of 56 Recce Regiment were to cross to Ripalto and take Chienti, the whole operation being supported by 17 Field Regiment RA. All went well and 5th Northamptons took over the defence of the town. During the night a heavy rainstorm broke, turning the country into a sea of mud and making movement off roads impossible. The country beyond Serracapriola appeared to be fairly good going for tanks and the brigade was ordered to continue the pursuit and seize the high ground overlooking the River Biferno. No opposition was met but progress was made very difficult by extensive demolitions and mines. By last light on the 2nd we had reached the line Portocannone — San Martino, which was taken over by 11 Brigade.

During this time the rest of the brigade was concentrating south of Foggia. 2nd Bn KRRC and 14 Light Field Ambulance came from Tripoli and we were joined by 98th Field Regiment RA, equipped with self-propelled 105 mm guns, who came from Fifth Army on the west coast. Leaving the Sharpshooters in reserve, Brigade HQ returned to the rest of the brigade. By October 5th the whole brigade, less the Sharpshooters and A Squadron of the Royals was complete near Lucera.

On the night of 4/5th, 11 and 36 Brigades of 78 Division had been counter-attacked on the far side of the Biferno. The Sharpshooters were ordered to support them. For two days a fierce battle was fought in which at one time the enemy got to within 400 yards of Termoli harbour, their objective. The Sharpshooters undoubtedly saved the situation. They lost 8 tanks and knocked out 6 before being relieved by 12th Canadian Tank Regiment.

On October 9th, 46th Royal Tanks were sent up to join 78 Division on the coast road: on the 22nd 50th Royal Tanks joined 8th Indian Division on the inland route through Larino. The remainder of the brigade joined the Sharpshooters south of Serracapriola on the 24th. On the 27th 98 Field Regiment joined 78 Division. 2nd Bn KRRC moved to Termoli to guard the FMC. On November 2nd Brigade HQ moved to five miles north of Termoli.

46th Royal Tanks had been supporting 78 Division who were facing the River Trigno, and 50th Royal Tanks had one squadron forward with 11 Indian Infantry Brigade, where they had done magnificent work, getting their tanks to places where it was hard to believe that a tank could possibly go. They were firmly positioned on a hill overlooking the River Trigno opposite Celenza, where they could only be supplied by mule.

On 3 November the battle of the River Trigno began. In a hard morning's fighting 46th Royal Tanks lost 7 tanks, accounting for 6 enemy tanks and 2 SP guns. Meanwhile from the ridge south of the Trigno, at least 20 enemy tanks and SP guns had been seen coming down the road from Vasto to San Salvo. They were accurately engaged. In the afternoon the Brigade Commander was sent for by the Army Commander and ordered to bring 44th Royal Tanks from Serracapriola and take charge of the armoured battle.

Plans were being made for an attempt to take the San Salvo ridge, when reports came in that the enemy had withdrawn, and 50th Royal Tanks were ordered on to the ridge. 44th Royal Tanks had moved up and were sent over the river, 46th Royal Tanks being left to reorganise and come into reserve. 5 Northamptons of 11 Brigade, supported by 50th Royal Tanks, with great determination over difficult country and in face of considerable opposition captured the high ridge south of Vaso. 2 KRRC were brought forward from Termoli.

The advance continued along the San Salvo — Vasto road, 44th Royal Tanks following 50th Royal Tanks to the west of the axis, covering the left flank. The intention of the brigade was that 50th Royal Tanks would support 36 Infantry Brigade on the coast road, while 44th Royal Tanks and 98 Field Regiment RA would support 11 Infantry Brigade on the axis Cupello — Scerni. On 5 November Vasto was entered by 46th Royal Tanks, who had taken over from 50th Royal Tanks: on the Cupello — Scerni axis 626 Field Squadron RE were to prepare a crossing over the River Sinello. The Sappers were unable to do this, but 44th Royal Tanks managed to get all their tanks over and advanced on to the high ground on the far side the next day and established a bridgehead.

On 7th November 11 Brigade moved on to capture Paglietta and Mt Calvo, the high ridge dominating the River Sangro. The next period was spent by 4th Armoured Brigade in collecting tanks and making plans for the assault on the River Sangro. On 16 November 46th Royal Tanks, much to the regret of the Brigade, received orders to rejoin 23rd Armoured

Brigade, leaving their tanks behind. This just enabled the other three regiments to be made up to strength.

Extensive reconaissances of the River Sangro and the ground immediately beyond it were made, but the weather was against us from the start: every time the ground showed signs of drying, down came the rain again, upsetting all precious plans. Meanwhile both divisions had been pushing elements across the River and the brigade was ordered to infiltrate tanks across. 2 KRRC, now under command of 8 Indian Division, had been ordered to occupy Mt Calvo on 15 November: after six very uncomfortable days there, they were ordered to attack and capture the "Castle" feature on the left of the escarpment held by 8 Indian Division. This was a strong and difficult position, well defended with dug-in positions: though they failed in the first attempt, they made no mistake the second time. The rain kept falling and the river rose at times to such heights and the current to such a strength that it was quite unfordable: as a result supply of those troops across the river became most difficult. Bridges were built under most difficult conditions. The first tanks across were of 50th Royal Tanks on 21 November, followed by 9 tanks of Sharpshooters on 22 November. Later a better crossing further up the river was found, but it was not until 28 November that we had a total of 124 tanks across.

The final Corps plan was for 8 Indian Division to attack up the Mozzagrogna road and for 78 Division, led as before by 4th Armoured Brigade, to pass through and mop up from Santa Maria to the sea. The attack was partially successful, 21 Brigade capturing Mozzagrogna; but every kind of evil device — mines, booby traps and demolitions — prevented 50th Royal Tanks from getting to them: counter-attacked by tanks and flame-throwers, they were forced to withdraw. Sharpshooters and 6 Inniskillings were to capture R. Li Colle feature as far left as Santa Maria and 44th Royal Tanks and 2 LIR were to pass through and mop up Fossacessia to the sea.

An extremely bad anti-tank ditch was encountered, but with great determination Sharpshooters kept trying, until eventually a way through was found: great credit is due to the Sharpshooters and 6 Inniskillings for their determination not to be beaten that day. 626 Field Squadron performed a heroic task in sweeping and marking lanes under most unpleasant conditions.

44th Royal Tanks eventually got through, going round by road through Mozzagrogna. On 30th November an extremely heavy barrage was opened on enemy defences in front of 44th Royal Tanks: as it lifted from block to block, a squadron of tanks and a company of infantry overran the area regardless of mines or ground, followed by another squadron and company on to the next block. The plan was entirely successful and the enemy was shattered and completely overrun. Fossacessia was entered and the area from there to the sea mopped up. By 30th November the entire Sangro position was in our hands, many Germans killed, some 300 prisoners and much arms, equipment and stores being captured.

The next objective was the big feature overlooking the River Moro. On 4 December 38 Bde took over the front, supported by 44th Royal Tanks. 44th Royal Tanks had some difficulty in crossing the river and it took all day to subdue the enemy on the feature. Sharpshooters made strenuous attempts to cross, but after 8 tanks had been bogged, further attempt was abandoned, Sharpshooters remaining in fire positions on the east of the river.

From now until the end of the month the Brigade remained in reserve under command 5 Corps, less 50th Royal Tanks under command 8th Indian Division and 44th Royal Tanks and 98 Field Regiment under 1st Canadian Tank Brigade and 1st Canadian Division respectively. Sharpshooters and 626 Field Squadron RE withdrew to the Treglio area for rest and repair while Brigade HQ moved to the old HQ of 65 German Division in Treglio.

At the end of December Brigadier Currie left the brigade to go home and take over the job of BRAC to First Canadian Army. He was succeeded by Brigadier H J B Cracroft, who had been commanding 12th Royal Tanks in North Africa. We were now told the great news that at last the brigade was to go to England for the first time in its history. 50th Royal Tanks left us to rejoin 23rd Armoured Brigade near Naples and the brigade moved to Lucera, where we handed in our vehicles and equipment and entrained for Taranto. Several days were spent in Taranto until we entrained again for Naples. Here we took command again, after a long absence, of the Royal Scots Greys. On January 27th 1944 we embarked on MV Tegelberg and HMT Almanzora and set sail for home.

On February 7th our convoy arrived at the "Tail o' the Bank" after an uneventful voyage. We steamed up the Clyde to the King George V Dock at Glasgow, where the Black Rats first set foot on the soil of the homeland. We went straight by train to Worthing, where we came under 1st Corps, settled into billets and went off on leave.

On March 16th Brigadier Currie returned to command us, Brigadier Cracroft transferring to 8th Armoured Brigade. We were re-equipped with Shermans, unfortunately not diesel, and got our first 17 pounder tanks. Discussions and training exercises were carried out mostly with 51st Highland Division, whom we expected to support when the great day came. June 1944 found us, as June 1943 had done, all teed up to set sail for an invasion.

CHAPTER V

Liberation — France, Belgium and Holland — June 1944 to February 1945

For the Invasion the Brigade was equipped with Sherman tanks again, though unfortunately not diesels. They were mostly the original Wright Whirlwind model, each regiment having twelve 17 pounder tanks for the first time. On June 6th, D Day, we began to move from the marshalling areas, embarking at Stokes Bay and anchoring in the Solent, listening with bated breath for the news of the assault on the beaches.

The first troops of the brigade landed on M beach at La Rivière at eight o'clock on the morning of June 7th under command of the Highland Division. The Sharpshooters were placed in support of 153 Brigade, one squadron supporting the 1st Bn The Black Watch in an abortive attack on the strongly fortified radar station of Douvres La Delivrande.

On the 8th rumours were current of an enemy counter-attack with tanks in the area of Coulombs, on the boundary between 1st and 30th Corps. The Sharpshooters moved to the high ground south of Creully where they joined hands with 1st Royal Tanks of 22nd Armoured Brigade, sent there to support 50th Division against the same mythical counter-attack which never developed.

Meanwhile The Greys had taken over support of 153 Brigade on the left. By June 10th all the fighting troops of the Brigade were ashore.

On the 11th we concentrated near Colomby-sur-Thaon, on the main road from Courseulles to Caen to support 9 Canadian Brigade of 3 Canadian Division against a supposed threat. The Sharpshooters took up fire positions among the infantry near Villons Les Buissons, the rest of the Brigade being on either side of Colomby. Main Brigade HQ in the chateau at Beny sur Mer was an obvious target for the enemy artillery and was finally forced to evacuate it on the 13th, after several direct hits had set the chateau on fire. From then till the 25th the Brigade was engaged in supporting 51st Highland Division and 3 Canadian Division in the same area.

On the 25th the Brigade, with 4 RHA now under our command, came under command of 11th Armoured Division in 8 Corps. On the 26th 15th Scottish Division had reached the line St Mauvieu to Cheux and 11th Armoured Division were passing through to seize a crossing of the river Odon. In the afternoon enemy tanks were reported at Rauray and the Brigade was called forward to support 29th Armoured Brigade. Brigadier Currie had just given orders to Commanding Officers at the level crossing south of Bretteville when he was killed by shellfire. By his death the Brigade lost a gallant and inspiring commander who had led them with great success and skill from Foum Tatahouine, by the Mareth Line, to victory in North Africa, through Sicily and Italy to the fields of Normandy. Lieut-Colonel Cameron, commanding the Sharpshooters, took over command until I arrived in the afternoon of the following day. By that time 29th Armoured Brigade, with 44th Royal Tanks also under command, had crossed the Odon near Baron: 159 Brigade were holding the area of the crossing and we were protecting both flanks between Cheux and the River, while 15th Scottish Division stepped up behind, taking over the ground gained by 11th Armoured Division. This situation lasted for three days. On the open high ground between the Odon and the Orne, 29 Armoured Brigade could make no headway against strong opposition from tanks and SP guns, 44th Royal Tanks losing 12 tanks on one day on the right flank. The Germans made constant efforts to penetrate both flanks of the narrow salient in the valley of the Odon and north of it, the situation on several occasions being extremely confused in the thick hedgerows of the Bocage. We continued to clear up and protect the flanks, supporting 159 Brigade and succeeding brigades of 15th Scottish Division and later 53rd Welsh Division, until the bridgehead over the Odon was securely established and contact made with the Canadians a few miles south-west of Caen. 11th Armoured Division were now withdrawn and on July 3rd we came under command of 53rd Division. 43rd (Wessex) Division then arrived to take over the area between the Canadians and Baron and we came under their command. On July 8th an attack by 43rd and 15 Scottish Divisions was launched to extend the bridgehead over the Odon towards the Orne, which we supported, though Churchills of 31st Armoured Brigade did most of the direct support of the infantry. This attack got no further than the outskirts of Evrecy and to Maltot: casualties were heavy particularly round Hill 112 and Maltot, the latter being eventually abandoned. For the next ten days we were engaged under command of 12 Corps in supporting 43rd and later 53rd Divisions in this area, which was a most unpleasant one. Shellfire was intense and accurate, and casualties to tank commanders were heavy. On July 20th we were withdrawn into reserve near Carpiquet aerodrome coming under command of 11th Armoured Division in 8 Corps. While we were there 3rd CLY amalgamated with 4th CLY from 22nd Armoured Brigade and became 3/4 CLY, the one and only Sharpshooters.

On July 28th we came under command of 2nd Canadian Corps. The Greys moved through Caen to support 4 Canadian Brigade of 2nd Canadian Division in the area of Ifs and Hubert Folie south of the town, again a very unpleasant area of accurate and heavy shell and mortar fire. One squadron was attacked one morning by a detachment of "Beetles", the German remote-controlled tanks, but none got as far as our tanks. On the 29th The Sharpshooters also moved to that area under command of 7th Armoured Division, on the left of The Greys, 4 RHA coming under 4th Canadian Armoured Division in the same area on the 30th. We had thought that we were going to take part in the Canadian attack towards Falaise, but on August 2nd we were placed under 8 Corps again and moved round to near St Paul Du Vernay, half way between Bayeux and Caumont. On the 4th we came under command of 3rd British Division, moving on the 6th to join them west of Beny Bocage. On the 8th The Greys were placed in support of 185 Brigade, Sharpshooters in support of 8 Brigade and 44th Royal Tanks with 9 Brigade in their attack over the River Alliere and on to the high ridge beyond, outflanking Vire from the east. After some fierce fighting, including crossing the river by Scissors Bridge and climbing an almost vertical slope beyond, 44th Royal Tanks captured the ridge with 9 Brigade, 8 Brigade with the Sharpshooters passing through on the right and The Greys with 185 Brigade on the left. After a short fight the enemy withdrew out of contact.

On August 12th we were relieved by a battalion of 6th Guards Armoured Brigade and moved again, this time by transporter, to join 12 Corps near our old battleground by Evrecy. On the following day we came under 53 Division and moved to a further concentration area east of the Odon round Mulrecy, D Squadron of The Royals coming under our command. On the 14th we moved up to Bois Halbout, Sharpshooters passing through 71 Brigade to the high ground beyond, while D Squadron of The Royals found a way through the thick woods to Bonnoeil, which was occupied by 2 KRRC with a squadron of 44 Royal Tanks by last light. On the 15th The Sharpshooters with two companies of 2 KRRC continued the advance through very thick "bocage" on the left of 44 Royal Tanks as far as Treprel, where determined resistance by enemy infantry, backed up by SP anti-tank guns, held them up until the afternoon, by which time 44 Royal Tanks had come up on their right, after dealing with the enemy on the west edge of Treprel. By last light 44 Royal Tanks, with one company of 2 KRRC, had cut the main road from Condé to Falaise, south-west of Treprel, and The Sharpshooters had done the same further east. During the night 6 RWF of 160 Brigade caught up with The Sharpshooters and helped to make the area secure and two companies of 4 Welch took over behind 44 Royal Tanks. On the 16th 160 Brigade took over the area we had captured and began to mop up and extend it, while The Greys supported 1 HLI on a cross-country move to Martigny and beyond. They continued to support them on the following day in seizing the high wooded ridge south-west of Falaise. Meanwhile the rest of the brigade concentrated behind 71 Brigade, ready to pass through when they reached the Falaise—Argentan road. This they did by a brilliant night attack down the ridge. Soon after first light the Greys, with one company of 2 KRRC, passed through 71 Brigade heading down the main road to Argentan. Near Ronai the leading squadron ran into a column of guns and horse-drawn transport which it dealt with effectively, but they continued to have considerable trouble from German tanks and SP guns to their front and open left flank. The Sharpshooters meanwhile had got down the steep wooded ridge further west, but were held up at a village covering the exit from the woods. 44 Royal Tanks, moving across country between the two, came up on the right of The Greys and were soon in action against enemy columns trying to move east. By last light the Sharpshooters had got one Squadron round behind the village of Rouffigny, but had not cleared it up, 44 Royal Tanks were on the edge of Ronai and The Greys on the outskirts of Pierrefitte. Each had their motor company with them. The woods and hedge rows were full of German infantry and there were a considerable number of German tanks and SPs about, trying to prevent us from closing the narrow gap between ourselves and Argentan.

On the 19th we pushed a little further south, The Sharpshooters clearing Rouffigny and 44 Royal Tanks clearing Ronai and taking 200 prisoners. We continued to inflict considerable damage on the enemy attempting to move east, which he now only dared do by single vehicles travelling very fast and by crawling up hedgerows. We were relieved by 71 Brigade in the afternoon and moved to the area of St Clair, coming under command of 15 Scottish Division, prepared to move south-east to clear up the final pocket between 53 Division and the Canadians. Plans were changed and on the 21st we came under command of 2 Canadian Corps to carry out the same task, 53 Division recce regiment being also placed under our command. In the afternoon 44 Royal Tanks and 2 KRRC supported by 4 RHA passed through 53 Division Recce. By last light our task had been completed with the capture of 3000 prisoners, and the "Falaise pocket" had been finally eliminated. We reverted to the command of 53 Division at midnight, but changed to 15 Scottish Division again next day, the 22nd. Between the 23rd and the 28th we moved from Trun to Ailly, on the west bank of the Seine, without opposition except from the mass of dead horses and derelict vehicles blocking every road. Here 4 RHA left us to go and re-equip with SP guns, being relieved by 6 Field Regiment. On the 29th we crossed the Seine at St Pierre du Vauvray, concentrating in the bridgehead formed by 15 Scottish Division, with D Squadron of The Royals again under our command.

At first light on the 30th we led 53 Division out of the bridgehead, our objective being Gournay. The Sharpshooters followed close on the heels of The Royals and little opposition was met. By last light we were beyond it on three sides, Sharpshooters to the north-west, 44 Royal Tanks to the north-east and Greys to the west, each with a company of 2 KRRC. During the night a column of Germans, escaping from Rouen, got astride the centre line between the Sharpshooters and their forward squadron which, with the Royals and a company of 2 KRRC, was holding the bridge three miles north of Gournay. This took some time to clear: meanwhile The Greys were advancing on a separate axis on the left. We were now under 7 Armoured Division, the rest of the division crossing the Seine behind 53 Division.

After The Sharpshooters had cleared Bazancourt and Villers Vermont, capturing 200 prisoners and knocking out a number of guns, 44 Royal Tanks passed through them, clearing each village on the axis in turn. Little opposition was met in Grandvilliers and, after completely destroying its flank guard, they came upon a dense column of transport trying to move through Poix. The Greys had found the tail of another column some six miles further west and both regiments began to inflict heavy punishment on the enemy. They were both low in petrol and ammunition: while they were refuelling, the Typhoons of the RAF were given a free hand with more German columns to the north, bringing all movement to a stop. Towards last light both regiments continued their advance, clearing a way through the carnage as best they could and halting after dark about six miles north of Poix. Our bag for the day had been 1500 prisoners, 5 guns and untold quantities of transport, motor and horse-drawn.

Our objective for the next day, September 1st, was a crossing over the Somme. 44 Royal Tanks on the right were directed on Picquigny, The Greys on the left to Longpre. Sharpshooters were following up the Greys protecting the open left flank between us and 4 Canadian Armoured Division. Both regiments met the enemy on the line of the road through Molliens-Vidame. This was soon dealt with and the advance resumed. Meanwhile Tac R reported that the Picquigny bridge was blown and 44 Royal Tanks were redirected to Ailly, further east. The bridge here was blown as they approached. The Greys found the main road bridge east of Longpre blown, but with great skill and dash seized the smaller bridge to the west before the enemy destroyed it. They managed to get two troops over, but the bridge itself was weak and there was a wet crater in the road this side of it: several attempts were made to improve it, but for most of the day the bridgehead in and around the village of Long was held only by two troops of tanks and a company of 2 KRRC. Every attempt by the enemy to get back to the bridge was foiled in spite of the thick country, and the rest of the squadron crossed by nightfall. The Sharpshooters on their left rear had made contact with the Canadians, leaving Airaines behind them still occupied by the enemy. This isolated party resisted strongly. Unfortunately Lieut-Colonel Littledale, commanding 2 KRRC, drove straight into the village and was killed instantly. The Sharpshooters made one attempt, with one company of 2 KRRC, to clear it from the north-west, but had not the men to complete it. Meanwhile we had been ordered to move round north of Amiens to secure an area north of the Somme in which 7 Armoured Division could concentrate during the night. Accordingly in the failing light 44 Royal Tanks, followed by Tac Bde HQ, crossed the river at the western outskirts of Amiens and continued in the moonlight to the high ground north of Canaples, twelve miles to the north. On the 2nd 44 Royal Tanks advanced to Bernaville, where, protecting the left flank of 7 Armoured Division, they completely destroyed a German column moving east, taking 600 prisoners. The Sharpshooters crossed the river at Picquigny and turned left clearing the north bank for fifteen miles and linking up with the Greys bridgehead at Long, destroying a battery of 88s on the way. For the next two days, under command of 12 Corps, we protected the left flank of the Corps axis, stepping up behind 53 Division and clearing the area to the west as far north as St Pol. On the 5th we returned to the command of 7 Armoured Division, moving behind 22 Armoured Brigade through Aubigny, Vermelles, Carvin and Seclin, crossing the Belgian frontier at Estambourg, finally halting with The Sharpshooters at Oudenarde, 44 Royal Tanks at Kerkhove and The Greys at Avelgem. We were ordered to remain concentrated there while 131 Brigade passed through. We had a completely open left flank, an area in which there were known to be large numbers of Germans, pressed from the south by the Canadians and Poles. During the night therefore I obtained permission from the commander of 7th Armoured Division to face west next day and protect the Corps axis from that direction. At first light the Brigade therefore took up battle positions on a front of fifteen miles on the high ground between the River Escaut and the Lys canal, the Sharpshooters covering Oudenarde, 44 Royal Tanks Kerkhove and The Greys Avelgem. It was not long before my suspicions were proved correct and a stream of Germans began moving east heading for the Escaut along the whole brigade front. With only one motor company with each regiment it was impossible to prevent infiltration through the villages and hedgerows. In spite of heavy losses the Germans continued to try and break through. All through the afternoon the tanks were sweeping their areas over and over again. It was clear that we could not hold them during the night on such a broad front. Luckily there was a road running east of the river which could be used as an alternative Corps axis, provided we held the bridge at Avelgem and kept the Germans from crossing the river anywhere. After warning the Divisional Commander of the situation and securing his agreement, regiments were pulled back at last light to the immediate vicinity of the bridges and Brigade HQ and all echelons moved east of the river. During the night the German 712th Division tried several times to reach the bridges but got no further than the main road between the villages. At first light on the 7th each regiment counter-attacked and drove the disorganized enemy back to the high ground. A large number of prisoners were taken and many casualties inflicted. The enemy made no further attempt to break out to the east and the second battle of Oudenarde was over. During the afternoon and night of the 7th we handed over the area to a brigade of 15 Scottish Division. On the 8th The Sharpshooters moved at first light to Antwerp to join 53rd Welsh Division there, while the rest of the brigade, including 4 RHA who had returned equipped with SPs and relieved 6th Field Regiment, concentrated south of Termonde by last light. We were still under command of 7th Armoured Division. Our task was to clear the area west of the Scheldt and north of the River Durne. 11th Hussars and Royals had patrols in the area but more and more Germans were flooding in from the north and west.

The Greys with 'C' Company 2 KRRC moved before last light on the 8th to take over Lokeren from one squadron of the Inniskilling Dragoon Guards. At first light the rest of the Brigade crossed the wooden bridge at Termonde, (later classified as capable of carrying 9-ton loads after considerable repair!), led by 44 Royal Tanks with 'B' Company 2 KRRC. No enemy were met and 44 Royal Tanks entered St Nicolas in triumph. Meanwhile 1 RB from 22nd Armoured Brigade had come under our command and had relieved The Greys in Lokeren. I had ordered the Greys to move to Beveren Waes, north-east of St Nicolas and on the opposite bank of the Scheldt to Antwerp. The rest of 2 KRRC came to take over St Nicolas before 44 Royal Tanks moved any further.

St Nicolas by this time was a scene of wild and delirious rejoicing. Crowds thronged the square and blocked the streets. In the middle of it The Greys, moving up the by-pass just east of the town, met a German column coming in the opposite direction. It had first opened fire on a recce party of 4 RHA. At the same time further German columns tried to enter the town from the north and north-east. The battle which followed had a sobering effect on the crowds for a time. By the middle of the afternoon the enemy had either been destroyed or withdrawn northwards and calm restored. On the 10th The Greys liberated Beveren Waes and met the enemy holding a strong position at Calloo and Fort Sainte Marie, on the bank of the Scheldt. Our object was to prevent the use of the ferry further north at Lillo. It was clear that a full scale attack would be necessary to capture Calloo, the approaches to which were completely open over boggy ground intersected with dykes. 1/7 Queens were put under my command for this and arrived during the afternoon. Everything was laid on for an attack at last light, but it had to be cancelled as the medium regiment was not forthcoming and the plan was changed, our area to be handed over to the Polish Armoured Division. The hand over took place on the 12th and we moved back to Termonde, the tanks having to go all the way round through Wetteren. Next day we moved on again to a concentration area around Boisschot, where we expected to get a few days for maintenance which was badly needed. Meanwhile the Sharpshooters had moved from Antwerp to Gheel, and were supporting 15 Scottish Division in forming and extending the bridgehead over the Junction Canal.

On the 17th September 44th Royal Tanks moved to near Hechtel, coming under command of 30 Corps. They were to link up with 101 US Airborne Division between Son and Veghel on the road from Eindhoven to Nijmegen. On the 18th the Brigade, less the Sharpshooters and 44th Royal Tanks moved to 8 Corps and took over from the Inns of Court Regt the line of the Junction Canal from Lanklaer to Bocholt, a front of 15 miles. On the 20th the Sharpshooters rejoined us, taking over the southern bit of the front from 2 KRRC: 1st Belgian Brigade took over from Bree northwards. By that time we had cleared all the enemy from the west bank of the canal.

The Arnhem operation started on September 17th: on the 20th 44th Royal Tanks joined up with 101 US Airborne Division and had a strenuous fight to keep the main road open. On the 22nd the enemy succeeded in cutting the road north of Veghel. 44th Royal Tanks successfully organised a counter-attack and the road was open again early on the 24th. On the 25th it was cut again south of Veghel and again 44th Royal Tanks cleared it. The Germans never succeeded in reaching the road again, though they remained quite close to it for a long time and the 44th Royal Tanks' anxieties were by no means over.

On the 26th, having handed over our front to the Royals, we took over from 8 Brigade of 3 British Division the area of Weert, a front of 12 miles along the Bois le Duc and Wessem Canals. We were faced by German parachute troops whose enterprising and aggressive patrols kept us busy every night. On October 3rd The Greys, relieved by 4th Tank Grenadier Guards moved up to Nijmegen coming under command 30 Corps for the support of 101 US Airborne Division on The Island. 44th Royal Tanks concentrated at Volkel for a few days' sorely needed maintenance. On the 6th the Grenadiers left us without relief, and The Sharpshooters and 2 KRRC held the entire front until we were relieved by 7 US Armoured Division on the 8th. The following day the brigade moved up to west of Nijmegen to join the Greys under command of 12 Corps, who had relieved 30 Corps. Next day The Sharpshooters crossed Nijmegen bridge to join 53rd Welsh Division and 44th Royal Tanks to join 50th Division, the Greys remaining with 101 US Airborne Division. On the 13th the brigade also took over from 157 Brigade the area between the Lower Rhine and the Maas, west of the Reichswald, 61st Recce Regt and the Royal Netherlands Brigade coming under our command and 2 KRRC manning the south bank of the Lower Rhine on the left flank of 101 US Airborne Division, who were on the far side. This state of affairs lasted until the night of October 17th when the whole brigade were relieved by 8th Armoured Brigade. On the 18th we moved to the area west of Eindhoven, The Royals and the Royal Netherlands Brigade also coming under our command. For the first 24 hours we were under the Highland Division but the following day came direct under 12 Corps. On that day 2 KRRC and 44th Royal Tanks took over the front north of Poppel from a brigade of 49 Division. We now had a brigade front of twenty miles from Eindhoven to where we joined hands with the Polish Armoured Division west of Poppel. The Sharpshooters were supporting the Royal Netherlands Brigade and the right squadron of The Royals, The Greys supporting the rest of the front of the Royals, 4 RHA and the 6 guns of the Royal Netherlands Brigade supporting the whole front. Between then and the 24th there was considerable activity in 2 KRRC's area, but only patrols elsewhere.

On the 25th, while 15th Scottish Division on our right was attacking westward north of the Wilhelmina Canal and the Polish Armoured Division on our left attacking north-west towards Breda, we attacked towards Tilburg on two axes, The Sharpshooters and the Royal Netherlands Brigade up the road from Hilvarenbeek, 2 KRRC and 44th Royal Tanks towards Goirle. Mines, demolitions and boggy ground held up both groups all day. On the 26th we were into the outskirts of Tilburg on the right and on the edge of Goirle on the left. During the night 44th Brigade of 15 Scottish Division relieved our right group, which moved round to Poppel. During the 27th 2 KRRC cleared Goirle finding more mines and demolitions and the Royals moved out on their left to fill the gap between them and the Poles. 4 GHQ

Tps RE, who were also under our command, finished building the bridge south of Goirle before last light and The Greys moved into the town after dark with one squadron of The Royals. At first light on the 28th, Tilburg having now been entered by 15 Scottish Division, The Greys and 2 KRRC moved through the western outskirts and west along the road to Breda. They regained contact with the enemy south of Rijen about ten miles west of Tilburg: the rest of the day was spent clearing Rijen and the woods to the south and south-west of it, while Royal Netherlands Brigade and The Sharpshooters moved up to take over the area astride the main road and the Royals kept touch with the Poles in the area of the aerodrome. Next day, leaving The Royal Netherlands Brigade, The Greys, 2 KRRC and one squadron of The Royals in the area of Rijen under command of 7th Armoured Division, the rest of the Brigade, with the Royals less one squadron, still under command moved all the way back to our old sector of the front near Weert, coming under command of 7 US Armoured Division in 8 Corps on arrival. We were joined there by The Greys, 2 KRRC and the remaining squadron of The Royals next day. On the 31st we came under command of 53rd Welsh Division who also had been hurried to this area to face the expected counter-attack which had already begun further north. By November 2nd The Royals had left our command and 53 Division had taken over the whole front, the Brigade being in Div reserve prepared to support all sectors, which we continued to do for the next ten days. On November 13th 12 Corps' Operation "Mallard" began to clear the enemy from west of the Maas. 44 Royal Tanks and the Vickers MGs of 2 KRRC fired a diversionary indirect shoot on the left flank before The Sharpshooters, supporting 160 Brigade, advanced by artificial moonlight at half past ten at night to the banks of the Wessem Canal. The terrific display of fireworks produced by The Sharpshooters and the flails and Crocodiles working with them was so successful that no opposition was met on the canal itself at all. The Class 40 bridge was not completed until half past seven on the evening of the 14th. 44th Royal Tanks were first across to support 158 Brigade near Baexem, followed by 4 RHA and The Sharpshooters, the latter supporting 160 Brigade in extending the bridgehead to either flank. The Greys with 71 Brigade crossed at nine o'clock on the morning of the 15th and reached the outer defences of Roermond, west of the river, before they met opposition, though mines were plentiful.

On the 18th we came under command of 49 Division to support their attack to clear the area beyond the Zig Canal up to Venlo. The brigade concentrated on the 11th on the road between Roggel and Meijel and on the 20th round Panningen. 44th Royal Tanks supported 146 Brigade on the right, The Sharpshooters in reserve ready to support 147 Brigade when they were used. The rest of the brigade advanced on the left of 146 Brigade, passing through 49 Div recce and taking them under command. During the 21st progress was slow owing to a large number of mines of all types, completely waterlogged ground and a few SPs which we could not locate. At first light on the 22nd 2 KRRC occupied Tongerloo, taking a few prisoners, and The Sharpshooters and 44th Royal Tanks supported their respective brigades up to the outer fringe of the western defences of Blerick, opposition being more determined on the 44th front, mines and bog being universal. 49 Div recce passed through 2 KRRC, who remained concentrated where they were, as did the Greys. 4 RHA moved up to an area east of Sevenum and came under command CRA 49 Division. On the 25th the brigade left 49 Division, except for 4 RHA and The Sharpshooters who remained to support them, and concentrated at rest south of Someren, joined there by The Sharpshooters on the 25th. 4 RHA on the 30th moved down to Hunsel, supporting 53 Division holding the line of the River Maas in that area.

This situation lasted until December 17th when the brigade came under command 11th Armoured Division in place of 29 Armoured Brigade who had gone away to re-equip. The armoured regiments stayed where they were, 2 KRRC taking over the line of the river from opposite Stevensweert to Wessem, the Inns of Court, also under our command, holding it south of them to Maeseyck, both supported by 4 RHA. Main Brigade HQ moved to Neeritter, leaving Rear HQ with the armoured regiments south of Someren. For the rest of the month we continued this task, a war of patrols, sniping and harrassing, snow adding to the interests and hazards of the job. On the last day of the year, 44th Royal Tanks, with a battery of 63rd Anti-Tank Regiment under command, relieved the Inns of Court. For the next fortnight patrolling became more active, both 2 KRRC and 44th Royal Tanks sending patrols over the river. On January 8th 'A' Squadron of 3/4 CLY, which had moved up for the purpose, took part in a highly successful attack by 8 Brigade of 3 British Division to destroy the enemy bridgehead west of the Maas at Wanssum.

On January 19th No. 3 Commando under our command crossed the Maas, captured Stevensweert and began to clear the Island between the Maas and the Juliana Canal, relieved the same day by 2 KRRC, a ferry being built at Stevensweert by 13 Field Squadron RE. On the 20th 2 KRRC completed clearing the island up to Maasbracht and made contact with 7th Armoured Division beyond the canal. By the 24th the advance of 7th Armoured Division on the far side of the Maas made our task superfluous and we were no longer in contact with the enemy. We remained in the same general area around Weert under command of 11th Armoured Division until February 17th, resting from our labours of liberation and training for the spring invasion of Germany.

CHAPTER VI

Into Germany to Victory — February — May 1945

At this time the brigade was still equipped with Sherman Is and IIs, but the proportion of tanks equipped with 17-pounders had doubled since D day, each regiment now having 24. Troops consisted now of two 75 mm and two 17-pounder tanks.

On February 18th, still as the armoured brigade of 11th Armoured Division, we moved to Tilburg, for the last time leaving the area of Weert, the hospitable inhabitants of which had made us regard it as our continental home. At the same time 14th Light Field Ambulance left us. They had been with us since July 1942, but henceforth independent armoured brigades were not allowed to have their own field ambulances. On the 23rd we moved by night across the Maas to a concentration area around Cleve. 11th Armoured Division were the right division of 2nd Canadian Corps and were to pass through Guards Armoured Division on the Goch—Calcar road directed south of Udem while 3rd Canadian Division attacked towards Udem from the north-west. The Sharpshooters were to be under command of 159 Brigade in exchange for 4 KSLI who were under us. At 6 o'clock on the evening of the 26th The Greys and 4 KSLI crossed their start line and soon made their first objective. After that opposition increased. They continued the attack with the aid of natural and artificial moonlight and after a hard night's fighting had reached the railway line south west of Udem by five o'clock in the morning with 150 prisoners, 4 SP guns and 2 tanks to their credit. By this time 3 Canadian Div had cleared all but the extreme south-west corner of Udem. At first light 44 Royal Tanks and 2 KRRC passed through The Greys and 4 KSLI. Progress was slow; the ground was very boggy, almost impossible for tanks, and there was only a gap of a few hundred yards between the anti-tank ditch round Udem and the thick woods, full of bazookas and infantry, supported by a few SPs, which ran all along our long open right flank. Shortly after mid-day The Sharpshooters with 3rd Monmouths under 159 Brigade began to pass through the Canadians to capture the ridge south-east of the town which overlooked the whole area we were fighting in. Considerable trouble was experienced with SPs, but by half-past four they had reached the upper slopes of the ridge, the 44th and 2 KRRC clearing the woods on the right flank and linking up with them. This they had completed at six, with the capture of 60 prisoners, Greys and 4 KSLI stepping up behind them to cover the approach to Udem from the south, which 3 British Div on our right had not yet reached. During that night and the following morning The Sharpshooters with 159 Brigade succeeded in forming a bridgehead over the stream beyond the ridge and extending it beyond, in spite of constant interference from SPs on the exposed right flank, which caused several casualties including the acting CO, Major Grey Skelton, who had taken over when Lt-Col. Bill Rankin was wounded on the 24th at a brigade "O group". In the afternoon of that day, March 1st, the brigade concentrated east of the stream, under cover of smoke, 4 RHA coming into action in full view of the enemy at a range of 1500 yards. At 1540 hrs the brigade attacked the Schliessen line in two groups. On the right 2 KRRC and 44 Royal Tanks, on the left 4 KSLI and The Greys. The ground was completely waterlogged and the whole area overlooked by the Hochwald and the high ground north of Sonsbeck. While the right group made slow but steady progress in spite of intense shellfire, SP anti-tank guns and pure bog, the left group came to a stop, the tanks completely bogged and the infantry unable to get forward in the face of intense MG fire from well-prepared defences. Further north however we had found a way into the line by a road which was over our boundary, but not being used by the Canadians on our left. The Greys got half a squadron and a company of KSLI there to hold the start line while the rest were extricated with difficulty and moved round behind them. This took till long after dark. Meanwhile the 44th and 2 KRRC had closed right up to the Schliessen line, but were still clearing woods on their long open right flank, which they continued to do during the night. At 3 o'clock on the morning of the 2nd, The Greys and 4 KSLI attacked southwards between the two lines of trenches on the edge of the forest. All went like clockwork: soon after first light they crossed the anti-tank ditch by Scissors bridge and captured the high ground on the edge of the forest overlooking the valley in which the rest of the brigade was. Here they defeated a counter-attack, which cost the enemy dear, and consolidated their gains, being heavily and accurately shelled all day. In the afternoon 2 KRRC and 44th cleared the southern end of the line in the face of bitter opposition, but had not completely cleared it by last light. This was done during the night and the following morning.

On March 4th 159 Brigade with The Sharpshooters passed through us and our battle of the Schliessen line was over. On the 7th we left 11th Armoured Division and moved to 12 Corps training area near Eysden on the Meuse in Belgium, to train for the crossing of the Rhine. 44th Royal Tanks were entirely re-equipped with amphibious tanks and spent a hectic ten days training in the River Meuse. We returned to the area of Sonsbeck and Udem on the 16th, the 44th coming up on the 22nd to a concealed assembly area near Xanten. We were now under command of 15 Scottish Division, who were to assault the Rhine under 12 Corps. They began their assault in Buffaloes of 33 Armoured Brigade in the early hours of March 24th. At 4 o'clock in the morning the 44th moved from their assembly area to a final forming up area by the river's edge on the extreme right of 15 Scottish Division's sector opposite the village of Bislich.

Shortly before half-past six they began to cross, their recce parties having crossed beforehand with the leading buffaloes. A few German MGs were still active on the left of the crossing area, but the only dangerous fire was from guns and mortars directed on the area of the crossing itself. By eight o'clock fifty-five of their tanks were over, four having been hit before entering the water and two in midstream. There they met up with the leading battalion of 46 Brigade, after helping 44 Brigade to clear the northern outskirts of Bislich. Turning north they cleared the east bank of the river between the two bridgeheads and went to clear the village of Meln. Throughout the 25th they were engaged in extending the bridgehead to the north and north-east, joining hands with 6 Airborne Division and one squadron coming under the latter's command. 4 RHA began to cross the river by raft in the afternoon and were all over after dark. During the night The Greys, 2 KRRC and Tac Brigade HQ crossed by the Class 40 bridge at Bislich which was receiving constant attention from the Luftwaffe. On the morning of the 26th The Greys and 2 KRRC under command of the brigade advanced north between 6 Airborne Division and 15 Scottish Division and opened up the road to Haminkeln against quite stiff opposition. The Sharpshooters with 44 Brigade came up on their right later in the day, 44 Royal Tanks, less the squadron with 6 Airborne Division, concentrating west of Haminkeln. The whole brigade was concentrated in this area by first light on the morning of the 27th, when we passed to command of 53rd Welsh Division to lead the advance towards Bocholt from Ringenberg, held by 157 Brigade under 6 Airborne Division. We had to wait for a Class 40 bridge to be completed, which it was at nine o'clock. The Greys and 2 KRRC passed through Ringenberg and were soon fighting enemy in the woods to the north of the town and the farms to the north-east. While they were clearing a start line for 160 Brigade astride the main road and pushing out to the north-east to the wooded high ground, The Sharpshooters grouped with 4 RWF, carried in Kangaroos of 49 APC Regt, attacked and cleared the ridge to the east of the high ground, taking several prisoners. Quickly exploiting their success, they made a bold dash through the thick woods and bogs, halting in the failing light about three miles south-east of Biemenhorst. 44th Royal Tanks supporting 160 Brigade were on the outskirts of Dingden by last light, their squadron which had been with 6 Airborne Division, supporting 158 Brigade on their left. Both groups continued the advance during the night: at first light The Sharpshooters and 4 RWF found themselves engaged in a fierce battle with enemy on all sides, supported by 88s forming the defence of Bocholt. As the 44th with 160 Brigade advanced beyond Dingden, Greys and 2 KRRC were pinched out and moved round to the east of The Sharpshooters and 4 RWF, clearing the woods on their right flank, from which they had had considerable trouble. At last light The Sharpshooters and 4 RWF attacked again and captured the road running east from Biemenhorst, the start line for 160 Brigade's attack on Bocholt that night, in which one squadron of The Greys took part.

Next morning 2 KRRC relieved 53 Recce Regt at Krechting and they and The Greys completed clearing up to the river, their one squadron continuing to help clear up Bocholt. The Sharpshooters joined 71 Brigade ready to pass through Bocholt and the 44th came back to us. At first light on the 30th the brigade passed through Bocholt directed on Rhede and Oding. The Greys and 2 KRRC formed the leading group followed by Tac Bde HQ and 4 RHA, 44 Royal Tanks in reserve grouped with 2nd Monmouths. Rhede was clear. A demolition beyond could not be crossed by Scissors: it was repaired by Sappers while Greys and 2 KRRC found a way round to the west and the 44th went round through the woods to the east. The Greys met only a few odd bazooka teams before meeting the 8th Hussars at Grosse Burlo. They and 1 RB were up against a determined party of enemy astride the road south of Oding, which was their objective as well as ours. We tried to find a way round to the left but struck nothing but impenetrable bog. We spent that night behind the 8th Hussars, watching our left flank. The following morning 8th Hussars and 2 Devons cleared Oding, Greys and 2 KRRC passing through heading north. After clearing some enemy from the woods north of the village, the road petered out and no more enemy were found. We now had orders to concentrate the brigade clear of Oding, which we did, The Sharpshooters with 71 Brigade having by now got beyond Vreden.

February to May 1945

On April 1st 2nd Mommouths left us, and the brigade moved by devious tracks with the help of a series of Scissors bridges to a further concentration area north-east of Winterswijk. By the end of the day The Sharpshooters, supporting 158 Brigade when they passed through 71 Brigade, had reached the edge of Gronau. Our task for the 2nd April was to diverge from the main axis beyond Vreden and clear the road to Epe then advancing on the right of 158 Brigade to Ochtrup, 1 HLI joining us north of Vreden in place of 2 Mons. Greys and 2 KRRC led again, meeting no opposition but a series of demolitions before reaching Epe. These were by-passed by the leading vehicles where possible, some crossed by Scissors bridge or by culverting. A number of concrete road blocks were met which were broken up by 17-pounder fire and then removed by tank-bulldozer. We had to wait for some time for the bridge to be completed at Epe, which it was in the late afternoon. The Greys recce troop had by then made contact with enemy south of Ochtrup and The Sharpshooters on our left were held up by a strong post covering the main road west of the town: Greys and 2 KRRC put in an attack at last light and continued after dark, clearing the high ground and built up area south of the railway. The 44th had meanwhile come up and taken over protection of their right rear. 1 HLI were brought up close behind in the first half of the night prepared to pass through 2 KRRC if we had to clear the whole town. We did not get a definite decision from the Welsh Division as to whether we or 158 Brigade were to clear it until after midnight. The enemy withdrew from Ochtrup during the night, 158 Brigade occupying it at first light. 160 Brigade passed through while we searched the area south of the town, clearing many mines and road blocks. The Sharpshooters returned to our command but remained with 158 Brigade ready to support them while The Greys moved to Neuenkirchen, supporting 160 Brigade in that area. A counterattack by 15 PG Division was expected from the north and the brigade less The Greys and 1 HLI, who had reverted to 71 Brigade, moved on the 4th to the high ground north-west of Wettingen in div reserve.

On the 5th we passed to the command of 52nd Lowland Division for the first time. The Greys, relieved by The Sharpshooters in support of 160 Brigade north-west of Rheine, moved through Rheine supporting 155 Brigade in forming a bridgehead over the Dortmund-Ems canal. By last light Brigade HQ was on the south edge of Rheine, 44th and 2 KRRC concentrated just north of the town. Soon after first light on the 6th The Greys were over the canal and up in Dreierwalde with 155 Brigade. While they continued the advance towards Hopsten, the brigade, with 44 Royal Tanks, 2 KRRC, 5 KOSB and 4 RHA under command, passed through 155 and 156 Brigades towards Spelle, carrier patrols of 2 KRRC having already reached the railway line. South of Spelle the enemy were holding a bridgehead which knocked out a recce patrol of 44th and was well supported by artillery and mortars from the north. There were a considerable number of Germans in the woods east of the canal, mostly from Gross Deutschland SS Panzer Training Battalion, but they were surprised by our appearance in their rear and gave little trouble. Shortly before last light 5 KOSB cleared the area south of the stream, supported by RAF Typhoons and a squadron of the 44th. Meanwhile The Greys with 155 Brigade were just south of Hopsten where there was considerable opposition. On the morning of the 7th 2 KRRC and 44 Royal Tanks tried to advance north towards Schapen. This proved impossible owing to bog and lack of bridges, but we managed to collect a number of prisoners and inflict damage on the enemy in the attempt. 155 Brigade had captured Hopsten during the night and it was now decided that the brigade should lead the advance to Halverde as soon as we could get through Hopsten, again a matter of boggy tracks until the bridges west of it were complete. 44 Royal Tanks and 2 KRRC were to lead, The Sharpshooters, now returned from 160 Brigade, being in reserve, grouped with 5 KOSB, neither yet relieved from watching the north flank between Hopsten and Spelle: Greys with 157 Brigade were to pass through towards Recke during the night. 44 Royal Tanks and 2 KRRC began their attack, by-passing Hopsten from the south, at about six o'clock. There was a considerable amount of shelling and a certain number of bazooka teams about. By dark they had reached the road east of Hopsten and continued their advance during the night by artificial moonlight to Halverde, taking about 40 prisoners. At first light The Sharpshooters and 5 KOSB in Kangaroos passed through Hopsten and continued the advance from Halverde to Weese. An enemy company at Weese were surprised by our appearance from the rear and were soon liquidated. Voltlage, two miles to the north, presented greater difficulties. The first tank to go up the road towards it was blown up near the bridge and every attempt to outflank met with impenetrable peat bog. 44 Royal Tanks and 2 KRRC meanwhile had moved round through Recke and tried to find a route forward to the right of The Sharpshooters, but without success. The Sharpshooters eventually found a way forward and attacked with 5 KOSB in Kangaroos, supported by RAF Typhoons at six o'clock. In spite of the fact that one company in Kangaroos took the wrong turning and drove straight into the middle of the village, all went well in the end. By nine o'clock the whole village had been cleared and was on fire after some stiff fighting which brought in over a hundred prisoners. Owing to the many possibilities of demolitions on the road north of Voltlage, the div commander decided to transfer the main thrust to the road further east leading to Uffeln. 52 Recce were in contact with a small party of enemy covering a bridge on this road. Unfortunately the road was cratered during the night: it was therefore some time before the 44th and 2 KRRC could get going on the morning of the 9th, though the carriers soon found enemy in the woods beyond the crater. For the rest of the day the 44th and 2 KRRC fought their way forward against the most determined resistance by Germans of a NCOs school from Hanover. Vinte was cleared by early afternoon and the final attack to clear Neuenkirchen went in about six o'clock. Meanwhile The Greys with 155 Brigade had relieved The Sharpshooters and 5 KOSB, who came round behind the 44th and 2 KRRC. At last light, the infantry carried in Kangaroos, they passed through Neuenkirchen and advanced unopposed by artificial moonlight to Uffeln.

156 Brigade relieved us during the night and the brigade, less The Greys who stayed behind under command of 52 Division, began a long move round to join 53 Division on the Weser. Tanks crossed the Ems-Weser Canal south of Vinte, wheels having to go all the way back through Rheine. Our route lay through Wester Kappeln, Halen, Veune and Welplage to Diepholz, Sulingen and Siedenberg to a concentration area round Asendorf, a move of over a hundred miles, much more for the weels. The first tanks got in just before dark, the rest of the brigade following all through the night. There we had two days maintenance and rest, both badly needed, The Greys rejoining on the evening of the 12th. Our future task was to cross the Aller at Rethem, as soon as the bridge there was complete, advance

up the road towards Walsrode to open up a gateway through which 7th Armoured Division could break out, and then swing north-west to outflank the enemy holding Verden. For this task we were to have 6 RWF in Kangaroos under command and The Sharpshooters were to support 158 and successive brigades of 53 Division in the direct advance on Verden down the east bank of the Aller.

As a result of constant and accurate shelling the bridge at Rethem was not completed until midday on the 14th. As soon as it was ready, 44 Royal Tanks and 2 KRRC crossed, securing Altenwahlingen and Kirchwahlingen with little difficulty. Resistance then became stiffer, the thick woods being full of German Marines armed with bazookas and spandaus and moderately well supported by artillery. Some progress was made, delayed by the necessity to pass through The Sharpshooters and a host of other units to join 158 Brigade to the north. By last light 44 Royal Tanks and 2 KRRC were half way to Eilstorf, and The Greys and 6 RWF were over the river and moving out to the right. After dark with the aid of artificial moonlight, 2 KRRC patrolled into Eilstorf while The Greys and 6 RWF drove straight through the enemy infested woods to the high ground east of the village. 4 RHA crossed the river and were in action round Altenwahlingen at first light, when the 44th and 2 KRRC began to clear Eilstorf and The Greys and 6 RWF attacked Kirchboitzen. Both attacks succeeded in the face of considerable and determined opposition, and the 8th Hussars, leading 22nd Armoured Brigade, were passed through the right flank of The Greys. We now swung north, The Greys and 6 RWF attacking Vethem and the 44th and 2 KRRC Sudkampen. There were a number of SPs about and both villages were defended with vigour. While Vethem was being cleared, one squadron of The Greys and two companies of 6 RWF slipped round it and by a quick dash across country reached Idsingen, 4 miles to the north, before dark, overrunning a number of guns. Meanwhile 44 Royal Tanks and 2 KRRC had cleared Sudkampen: by artificial moonlight they continued the advance to Nordkampen and cleared that too. Our total bag of prisoners for the day was 16 officers and 539 other ranks, all of the redoubtable 2nd Marine Division: many more had been killed.

At first light on the 16th the 44th and 2 KRRC began to clear the road up to Idsingen while the rest of The Greys and 6 RWF joined them at Idsingen, followed by Tac Brigade HQ and 4 RHA. Continuing the advance northwards The Greys found the bridge on the road to Groote Heins blown and defended. A scissors bridge was put down and one squadron and a company in Kangaroos crossed before the bog became impassable. 44th and 2 KRRC advanced north-east from Idsingen while an improvised bridge was built over the ruins. This was completed by two o'clock, by which time The Greys were on the main road south of Bendingbostel, which was strongly held. 44th and 2 KRRC were relieved by 53 Recce and began to concentrate behind The Greys. Bendingbostel was attacked in the late evening and Greys and 6 RWF had cleared it and seized a bridge to the west by last light. 44th and 2 KRRC then passed through them by artificial moonlight and attacked Klein Sehlingen and Kreepen, both of which had been cleared by first light, though there were still a large number of enemy in the woods all round. Relieved by 53 Recce Regt, The Greys and 6 RWF passed through the 44th and 2 KRRC at Kreepen and moved straight across country with little opposition to cut the main road north of Verden. During the day large numbers of prisoners were collected from the woods we had encircled or passed through, culminating in a haul of 273 by 4 RHA. During all this time The Sharpshooters had been supporting all the brigades of 53 Division in turn, entering Verden with 71 Brigade at about the same time as The Greys reached its northern outskirts.

On the 18th 6 RWF left us and The Greys joined 52 Division, who were to continue the advance to Bremen. The brigade, consisting only of 44 Royal Tanks, 2 KRRC and 4 RHA began to advance north at first light. Kirchwalsede was captured without difficulty, but Westerwalsede was found to be strongly held, a complete battery of 88s covering the approaches from south and east. By an encircling movement on both flanks the north edge of the village was entered with little difficulty, but a stiff fight ensued before it was entirely cleared up. Pushing on to the north, a line of guns was found covering the only crossing over another boggy stream. This was attacked in the afternoon with complete success and the bridge over the railway beyond captured intact. Continuing after dark 2 KRRC and the 44th captured the main road bridge over the railway and the important cross roads in the woods to the south. 9 Officers and 403 other ranks were captured and four 88s and nine 105s captured or destroyed. Next morning the cross roads became very lively with a SP firing direct on to it and infantry counter-attacking through the woods. By midday however the woods had been cleared and our hold on the area extended in all directions. In the afternoon we were relieved by 158 Brigade, with whom were the Sharpshooters, and moved back to an area northeast of Verden to come under command of 52 Division again. In the six days since crossing the River Aller the brigade had completely defeated most of the 2nd Marine Division, capturing 39 guns and a mass of equipment. We had fought day and night without stopping, advancing thirty miles against the continuous opposition of some of the best troops the Germans could muster.

The Sharpshooters remained with 53 Division. On the 20th The Greys were supporting 156 Brigade round Etelsen and the 44th supported 157 Brigade on their right, in capturing Volkersen, while 2 KRRC took over the right flank astride the main road to Rotenburg. On the 21st The Greys continued the advance with 156 Brigade against stiff opposition, the 44th with 157 Brigade coming up on their right through the woods. Shellfire was heavy and there were a large number of 88s and nebelwerfer about. The Sharpshooters with 53 Division were approaching Rotenburg from the south. On the 22nd the 44th supporting 157 Brigade had a fierce battle all day against the mass of 88s and 20 mms forming the outer anti-aircraft defence of Bremen. By the end of the day they had reached their objectives north of Achim after some tough fighting. On the 23rd the 44th extended to the north, cutting the autobahn and capturing Oyten, while The Greys supported 155 Brigade advancing west from Achim, which had been captured during the night. 2 KRRC meanwhile were stepping up covering the right flank between 52 and 43 Divisions. On the 24th The Greys continued the steady advance towards Bremen, supporting 157 Brigade up to the railway at Malendorf. This really finished the serious fighting for Bremen. On the morning of the 25th The Greys supported 156 Brigade and later 155 Brigade right into the heart of the city, the main trouble being rubble from the recent bombing, though odd panzerfaust parties were a nuisance. On the morning of the 26th, the 44th supported 157 Brigade passing through into the dock area, no opposition being met at all. We remained in Bremen until the 28th, when we joined 51st Highland Division near Bassen on the autobahn east of Bremen.

February to May 1945

We were to have helped them in their advance to the north, but there were no bridges and we moved again late in the day to Eversen on the road from Verden to Rotenburg ready to rejoin 12 Corps next day. On the 29th The Sharpshooters rejoined us, having supported all and sundry in 53 Division in clearing up the area round Rotenburg, and we set off on one of our long treks, mostly by track to save the cobbled roads. On arrival in the area of Salzhausen, twelve miles south of Winsen, the Brigade, less The Greys, came under 53rd Division again, The Greys coming under command of 6th Airborne Division in 8 Corps en our right. On of any 1st the Greys began to cross the Elbe with 6th Airborne Division at Lauenburg and one squadron of The Sharpshooters also crossed with 1st East Lancs of 158 Brigade. Events were obviously moving fast, but in spite of that we were amazed to hear that The Greys had met the Russians at Wismar, each squadron supporting a brigade of 6th Airborne Division. They had travelled without stopping all day as fast as their tracks would carry them, heedless of the crowds of Germans withdrawing in front of the Russians. On the 3rd the remainder of The Sharpshooters crossed the Elbe at Geesthacht and drove unopposed into Hamburg with 158 Brigade on the morning of the 4th. The rest of the brigade moved later in the day and occupied Bergedorf, between Geesthacht and Hamburg.

At eight o'clock on the morning of May 5th 1945 all opposition on the front of 21st Army Group ceased. So for 4th Armoured Brigade finished five years of fighting during which we had seldom been out of the line. Egypt, Libya, Tunisia, Sicily, Italy, France, Belgium, Holland and Germany had been our battlefields. The sign of the Black Desert Rat will we know be remembered by many people of many lands; by our enemies we hope with respect: by our friends we trust with gratitude and affection, as we remember them.

APPENDIX A

BRIGADE COMMANDERS

January 1940 to April 1941 — Brigadier J. A. L. Caunter. DSO, MC
(Royal Tank Regt)

April 1941 to April 1942 — Brigadier A. H. Gatehouse, DSO, MC
(Royal Tank Regt)

April 1942 to July 1942 — Brigadier G. W. Richards, CB, CBE, DSO, MC
(Royal Tank Regt)

July 1942 to September 1942 — Brigadier W. G. Carr, DSO
(12th Royal Lancers)

September 1942 to November 1942 — Brigadier M. G. Roddick, DSO
(10th Royal Hussars)

November 1942 to January 1943 — Brigadier C. B. C. Harvey, DSO
(10th Royal Hussars)

January 1943 to February 1943 — Brigadier D.S. Newton-King, DSO
(4th South African Armoured Car Regt)

February 1943 to December 1943
and March 1944 to June 1944 — Brigadier J. C. Currie, DSO, MC
(Royal Artillery)

December 1943 to March 1944 — Brigadier H. J. B. Cracroft, DSO
(Royal Tank Regt)

June 1944 onwards — Brigadier R. M. P. Carver, DSO, MC
(Royal Tank Regt).

APPENDIX B

UNITS OF THE BRIGADE

This list does not include all units which have ever served in the brigade but gives the official composition of the brigade at different times, excluding Headquarters 4th Armoured Brigade and 4th Armoured Brigade Signals.

1. January to May 1940
    - 1st Royal Tank Regiment
    - 6th Royal Tank Regiment

2. May to October 1940
    - 7th Hussars
    - 6th Royal Tank Regiment

3. November 1940 to February 1941
    - 7th Hussars
    - 2nd Royal Tank Regiment
    - 6th Royal Tank Regiment

4. May—June 1941
    - 4th Royal Tank Regiment
    - 7th Royal Tank Regiment

5. August 1941 to February 1942
    - 2nd Royal Horse Artillery
    - 2nd Bn The Scots Guards
    - 8th Hussars
    - 3rd Royal Tank Regiment
    - 5th Royal Tank Regiment
    - 5 Company, Royal Army Service Corps

6. April 1942 to July 1942
    - 1st Royal Horse Artillery
    - 8th Hussars
    - 3rd Royal Tank Regiment
    - 5th Royal Tank Regiment
    - 1st Battalion King's Royal Rifle Corps
    - 5 Company R.A.S.C.

7. August 1942 to May 1943

The composition of 4th Light Armoured Brigade was constantly changing but the following were generally part of it.

> 3rd Royal Horse Artillery
> The Kings' Dragoon Guards
> The Royal Dragoons
> The Royal Scots Greys
> 4/8th Hussars
> 11th Hussars
> 12th Royal Lancers
> 1st Bn King's Royal Rifle Corps (up to January 1943)
> 2nd Bn King's Royal Rifle Corps (after January 1943)
> 5 Company R.A.S.C.
> 14th Light Field Ambulance R.A.M.C.

8. July to August 1943. Sicily.

> 'A' Squadron The Royal Dragoons
> 3rd County of London Yeomanry (Sharpshooters)
> 44th Royal Tank Regiment
> 2nd Bn King's Royal Rifle Corps
> 5 Company R.A.S.C.
> 14th Light Field Ambulance
> 318 Armoured Brigade Workshops R.E.M.E.

9. August 1943 to January 1944

> As above with addition of
> 46th Royal Tank Regiment
> 50th Royal Tank Regiment
> 98th Field Regiment Royal Artillery (Surrey and Sussex Yeomanry)

10. February 1944 to May 1945

> 4th Royal Horse Artillery (joined June 1944)
> The Royal Scots Greys
> 3rd County of London Yeomanry (Sharpshooters) (became 3/4th C.L.Y. in July 1944)
> 44th Royal Tank Regiment
> 2nd Bn King's Royal Rifle Corps
> 5 Company R.A.S.C
> 14th Light Field Ambulance
> 4th Armoured Brigade Workshops (originally 318)
> 4th Armoured Brigade Ordnance Field Park
> 271 Forward Delivery Squadron R.A.C.

www.ingramcontent.com/pod-product-compliance
Lightning Source LLC
Chambersburg PA
CBHW061419090426
42743CB00027B/3499